PRAISE FOR *PROFITING FROM FORESIGHT*

Wow! This could be the basis for an executive MBA course.

—John Kozlowski, MBA, Managing Director, Partner Pathways

Scott Barnett, an experienced businessman, offers a valuable seven-point plan for increasing foresight so essential for business success. Logically organized and sprightly written, this account raises very important issues for business practitioners to consider. A lot to think about -- chock full of ideas. Those in marketing will find Scott's ideas particularly valuable.

—Mansel G. Blackford
Author of: *The Rise of Modern Business; Pioneering A Modern Small Business; and Business Enterprise in American History*
Professor (Emeritus) of History
The Ohio State University

The pace of change, driven predominately by new technologies and creative applications of those technologies, can be daunting and 'not for the faint of heart'. All levels of business need to be open to change and it will take leadership throughout the organization to be forward looking. In that regard, this is a very interesting read and perspective of foresight versus traditional methods used by management. Well-written with excellent examples and concepts.

—Andy Fulton, President, ME Global, Inc.

This is advanced material, very helpful to experienced business people.

—Randy Kravitz, MBA, Executive Director, Goldman Sachs 10,000 Small Businesses

Scott Barnett has the gift of long-range thinking, as well as skills to see all the way through challenges toward a desired outcome. In this profound yet practical book, Scott guides the rest of us to broaden our vision and reach our business goals.

—Diane Overgard, Executive Life Coach

A great read filled with actionable ideas that any individual or organization could implement to move their business forward.

—Robert Kocur, CFA, MBA
Investment Manager, Bell & Anderson

PRAISE FOR SCOTT BARNETT

Scott Barnett is a master at devising winning sales and marketing strategies. Even in highly competitive markets he's created a significant edge that attracts new customers. Scott has high integrity and meets his commitments.

—Rob Juncker, Winner Tekne Award, presented by the Minnesota High Tech Association (MHTA) in recognition of outstanding technology achievement and leadership.

I worked with Scott Barnett in a turn-around situation that became highly successful. Scott helped me to redefine the direction of the company, and with limited resources captured significant new business. He has very strong strategic marketing ability.

—Thomas Yeager

Scott Barnett has a talent for finding unmet customer needs. And with that he conceives new ways to add value to products and services. I worked with Scott for many years and he helped my business greatly.

—Pat Hetherington

I've known Scott Barnett for 15 years in my capacity as a corporate board member. He has impressed me with his ability to gain insights from the market and translate them into new product feature advantages. He also relates well to the needs of sales people and is effective at providing them tools to win more business.

—Dave Anderson

Scott Barnett is very skilled at strategies in IT and industrial product markets. Based on my many years of experience, he has a rare talent.

—Tom Brothers

We have used the consulting services of Scott Barnett on two strategic marketing projects. Scott is definitely an expert in high technology products and markets. We are extremely pleased with the results he has delivered. The biggest benefit is that Scott quickly gave us new insights about our markets that would have been difficult to realize otherwise. He enhanced our business development, uncovered competitors' weaknesses, and identified new market segments for us to enter.

—Dr. Dominik Kramer

PROFITING FROM FORESIGHT

PROFITING
FROM
FORESIGHT

A 7-STEP METHOD TO CAPITALIZE ON
THE EMERGING TRENDS OF THE FUTURE

SCOTT BARNETT

New Insights Press

Editorial Direction and Editing: Rick Benzel Creative Services
Page design and typesetting: Mayfly Design
Cover concept: Rick Benzel
Published by New Insights Press, Los Angeles, CA

First edition
Printed in the United States of America
Library of Congress Control Number: 2017954755
ISBNs: 978-0-9973357-5-0 (pbk); 978-0-9973357-6-7 (eBook)

For Becky, my wife and best friend

Contents

Acknowledgments

I WOULD LIKE TO THANK PEOPLE WHO ENCOURAGED ME, AND ASSISTED me with the writing of *Profiting from Foresight*. Early on my daughter Kelsey Barnett, award-winning student, writer and sounding board made important suggestions as did my father, James Barnett, former senior executive and business school dean. The enthusiasm of John Kozlowski, friend, former co-worker, and consultant was a big inspiration. My friends Randy Kravitz, Executive Director of Goldman Sachs 10,000 Small Businesses, Andy Fulton, president of ME Global, and Diane Overgard, executive coach gave helpful advice. Rick Benzel was awesome with his professional guidance editing and publishing the book. And finally, my late mother, Joyce Wortman Barnett, who I always remember for her courage and love.

Introduction

THIS BOOK OFFERS A METHOD FOR DEVELOPING ONE OF THE MOST valuable business skills—foresight to spot the trends of the future. It is also one of the most difficult skills to attain.

Foresight is what leads us to progress. All great opportunities for new products, new ventures, and new enterprises have resulted from foresight. The good news is that foresight can be learned and developed with training and practice. There is a method to it, and that is what this book will teach you.

Foresight has arguably become the most important ability we need to succeed in business—and in life. The pace of change in technology and society has accelerated to a point where we cannot live with the expectation that things will continue to stay the same on a steady course. We must transcend the ordinary, the generic, and a slow incremental view of progress if we want to truly thrive. Having foresight leads us on an upward path and shows us how to adapt. We can look out two years, five years, ten years or longer with greater understanding and purpose.

Upward is our desired potential and reverent direction. It's the connection to creativity, amazement, novelty, as well as to providence. Foresight comes from being active in the flow of things. It comes from the combination of skills of observing, discussing, researching, prototyping, hypothesizing, finding patterns, making notes, sketching ideas, experimenting, and testing. Far from being a solitary endeavor, it is more like a sport, where you collaborate with teammates, and wrangle with the world at large to win.

Once we have foresight, we must act, or more accurately, adapt. Adapting requires insight about behaviors and power structures "out there" in the real world. It calls for taking measures that will cause effective stage-setting moves. Thoughtless action will ultimately deter us from achieving such developments.

It is only possible to improve our foresight if we use a method; we don't want to wander aimlessly. The way of thinking in the method this book teaches you is influenced by process-relational philosophy, because it has the best

Tis easy to see, hard to foresee.

—Benjamin Franklin

approach to understanding change as a fundamental aspect of our lives.[1] Heraclitus said 2,500 years ago that you can't step into the same river twice; one of his students built on that idea, and said that you can't even step into the same river once. We, and the river, change even as we step into it. The key elements of process-relational philosophy relevant to business are:

1. Experience is constantly emerging
2. Everything is interconnected, and
3. Progress is transcendence of the obvious

Keeping these elements in mind, we are always looking at the emerging potential of our part of the world—the interconnectedness of people, ideas, and experiences; going beyond the obvious to think dynamically, not linearly; and adapting our behavior and actions to actualize our best vision of the future.

Defeating the Forces that Block our Path to Foresight

At one time or another, most of us have left behind a promising opportunity because we did not act. We may have felt that we did not have sufficient foresight to see what that opportunity really meant to us. With foresight, we would have had a lens to envision the possibilities that might have become actualized in the future with that opportunity.

You should also make things happen.
Why talk so much of inspiration?
Delay won't make it flow, you see.

—Faust, Goethe

What can often get in our way is when change is seen as threatening. To be on that path, we must defeat stubbornness, fear, and indecisiveness. We tend to avoid change. It may require new language and new meanings. Think of all the new vocabulary and concepts that have come about in just the last 20 years. Tweeting, Googling, blogging, the internet of things, deep learning, artificial intelligence, augmented reality, friending/unfriending, textspeak, etc. At first these were alien concepts, just as the internet was to most people 30 years ago. Many people resisted the internet at first, including Bill Gates.

To make progress we must put aside fear, embrace change in a new light, and recognize that conflict with the status quo is a necessary part of the process. In doing so, we can take steps to make the conflict constructive, not destructive.

All experience flows; there are no unchanging qualities. Our job is to better foresee the upward paths, and adapt to them. And, in looking upward to know that providence will help us along the way once we commit to it.

Overview of the Foresight Method

I wrote this book from a wide-ranging business background in market research, product management, marketing and sales management, consulting, and entrepreneurship. I've worked in and with all sizes of companies in a variety of industries, mostly related to technology. Like many people, I've wrestled with dramatic change, learning from problems I've seen along the way.

These are complicated times for businesses. Customers are becoming more self-directed, and more digital in their ways of doing things. Their expectations are greater, but they are less willing to pay premium prices. Perhaps you are facing pressing market issues and new threats. Your products might be fatigued, becoming more commodity like. Or, you feel like there are roadblocks stopping you from breaking through the logjam. You want to reinvent, transform, and launch, not accept the status quo. This book can help you with a rigorous method to channel your drive to improve and grow.

This book is organized into two Parts.

- In Part 1, the first five chapters provide pre-requisite knowledge and lay the groundwork for effective implementation of the method.
- In Part 2, I will walk you through the 7 steps that will guide you to better foresight:
  > Step 1: Start with intensive observation and discovery
  > Step 2: Scout the market terrain
  > Step 3: Define venturesome ideas
  > Step 4: Methodically rate and rank the best ideas
  > Step 5: Adapt the best emerging ideas to test the market
  > Step 6: Calculate risks and rewards before going all in
  > Step 7: Make a successful market entry

Who Will Benefit from This Book

More than being intended for a particular industry type or size of business, this book is meant to be a tool for executives and managers who are driven to achieve a new upward path for the business and themselves. It is useful to anyone involved in leading change, especially marketing executives, product managers, innovation heads, and entrepreneurs. My goal is to offer a method to improve your vision of what is possible and to show you how to develop more

Business, more than any other occupation, is a continual dealing with the future; it is a continual calculation, an instinctive exercise in foresight.

—Henry R. Luce, magazine magnate, co-founder and editor-in-chief of Time, Inc.

purposeful plans of action to capitalize on emerging opportunities. In doing so, you aren't looking just to survive, you want to thrive. Change is ongoing, not a part time job; it can't be done in fits and starts, or relegated to a back burner waiting for when you are ready.

How to best organize for innovation is a major dilemma in many companies, which this book will also discuss. It is often an obstacle to making progress. The organization's culture, its openness, its use of top down vs. bottom up management styles, and other issues play a part in making innovation happen.

Why This Book is Different

There are great books about innovation, creativity, and strategy, but, these activities must originate from foresight to be effective. It is critical to make the right kinds of innovations and develop the right kind of plans—and this only happens if you have foresight. That is what this book speaks to.

Unlike traditional methods, the foresight method is agile in recognizing emerging opportunities and adapting to capitalize on them. It offers a blueprint to organize, collaborate, and execute to win the markets of the future, and to keep your team focused only on the most highly promising opportunities. The foresight method is totally about results, not creating reams of paper plans that sit on a shelf and are out of date by the time they are printed. Agile teams, projects, and objectives are needed to deal with the volatile, uncertain, chaotic, ambiguous (VUCA) business world of today.

The ideas in this book will not be readily accepted by many businesspeople, especially those who have internally-focused responsibilities such as finance, administration, legal, accounting, HR, operations, etc. It will thus be important for you to take time to get others onboard, and to respond to their concerns. They are typically most concerned with: risk of financial loss, change in general, loss of focus, and pressure for short-term results.

You will need to persuade them that it is equally risky not to innovate, and that you agree with them that it is important to reduce risk. But assure them that your intention is to do just that, by methodically screening the best quality ideas and testing them. Regarding your time, effort, and focus, you will need to negotiate an arrangement with leadership, and communicate regularly about results of your work to maintain momentum.

Innovation isn't for the faint of heart, and you can't do it alone. This book will give you practical ideas to be a driver of innovation in your organization, and to encourage others to join your efforts. So, let's get started!

"Understanding, undirected and unassisted, is unequal to and unfit for the task" of overcoming major challenges.

—Francis Bacon, originator of the scientific method, author of Novum Organum (New Instrument of Science)

PART 1

The Grounding Behind the Foresight Method

1

Why You Need a Method

I ONCE WORKED AT A MARKETING CONSULTING FIRM, FRANK LYNN & Associates, in Chicago. Frank was wise and had developed an impressive roster of Fortune 500 clients. I was given the opportunity to present a talk to the staff of 30 consultants and partners on the topic of "Strategic Method." I spoke about a method of strategic planning that could benefit our clients and our company. After the presentation, Frank asked, "Why is having a method important?" Great question! (I said he was wise). I tried to give my reasons, but I didn't answer it very satisfactorily, and I knew it.

Now, years later, I believe I have a better answer. A method guides you how to follow one thing through to another. It drives and connects your train of thoughts, your observations, and speculations. In other words, it helps you to develop insight about cause and effect, which leads to foresight.

The driving principle of foresight is "speculative reason." This is the pursuit of the unattainable, a quest to approach the ideal. There is an element in our nature that drives us to reason speculatively through questions:

- How can the status quo be improved upon?
- What assumptions are no longer working?
- What new technological capabilities are likely to become available and how can they be useful?
- What newly emerging threats and risks do we need to be concerned about?
- What market trends do we expect to accelerate? What market trends are fading?
- In what ways are our customers changing?

Knowledge is of little use, when confined to mere speculation.

—Benjamin Rush, Founding Father, Civic Leader, Physician, Reformer

3

- In what ways might we need to adapt our business platform and business model?
- In what ways can we make our products and services more novel, unique, and useful?
- What will be the greatest growth opportunities for the future?

We must use a method to answer these questions. A method is a "mind tool" to improve our potential intelligence. It creates the capacity to look ahead. It helps us advance by asking, "What should I think about next?" before asking, "What should I do next?" As John Holland, the brilliant complexity science pioneer, put it:

> An internal model allows a system to look ahead to the future consequences of current actions, without actually committing itself to those actions. In particular, the system can avoid acts that would set it irretrievably down some road to future disaster ("stepping off a cliff"). Less dramatically, but equally important, the model enables the agent to make current "stage setting" moves that are obviously advantageous.

Foresight requires curiosity to understand why things are the way they are. The action it leads to is a "generate-and-test" approach to a premise or working hypothesis, followed by determination of the best way to adapt to the validation or invalidation of the premise.

The foresight method is independent of any belief system. It is neither judgmental nor indifferent to the present. It is based on the principle that at any time, a variety of paths are open to us, and some paths are better than others. The laws of nature dictate what's possible in any given circumstance. The laws don't determine any values, they are neutral in that sense. However, they do affect the values that are possible. Goethe, the great German writer, scientist, and statesman (1749-1832) said it well:

> Until one is committed, there is hesitancy, the chance to draw back. Concerning all acts of initiative (and creation), there is one elementary truth, the ignorance of which kills countless ideas and splendid plans: that the moment one definitely commits oneself, then Providence moves too. All sorts of things occur to help one that would never otherwise have occurred. A whole stream of events issues from the decision, raising in one's favor all manner of unforeseen incidents and meetings and material assistance, which no man could

have dreamed would have come his way. Whatever you can do, or dream you can do, begin it. Boldness has genius, power, and magic in it. Begin it now.

I agree with Goethe, because I have experienced the stream he talks about. However, I would add that you need foresight to commit to an upward path. I have also experienced an unfortunate stream of events by committing to a venture that went sour. Looking back, I can see that I forced this venture to make sense, and didn't do the work of the foresight method.

Comparing the Foresight Method to Traditional Analysis

A common theme I see in companies that fail is a lack of foresight into the possibilities of emerging opportunities (and threats), as well as a lack of a method of organizing to discover, capture, and adapt to them. Here are the differences between the typical analysis and innovation method versus the foresight analysis method. They are, in many respects, polar opposites:

Vision without action is a daydream.
Action without vision is a nightmare.

—Japanese Proverb

Typical Analysis and Innovation Method	Foresight Method
Passive	Assertive
Aloof, done in a silo	Engaging, collaborative
Numbers focused	Discovery and insight-oriented
Industry focused	Market/customer focused
Historical trends	Emerging trends
Status quo, defensive	Driven toward change, innovation
Risk avoiding	Risk reducing
Budgeting	Envisioning
Managing within a paradigm	Leading to a new paradigm
Closed feedback system	Open feedback system
Linear thinking	Dynamic, nonlinear thinking
Incremental	Exponential
Main-street focused, late to the game	Early-adopter focused, leading the game

What would you imagine about the innovative capabilities of a company that operates out of the left column above? Of the two columns, which one do you sense offers a brighter future?

Why We Need to Adapt

In chess, a good move usually has many purposes, but one thing is always true: It is bad to be passive. Good players make their pieces active. They put pressure on their opponents. In chess, the best defense is a good offense.

—Bryan Quick, Executive Director of the Marshall Chess Club

Change is ever-present. Yet we are seeing pushback in parts of society to the rapid changes in our times. Technology and the globalization of commerce have sped ahead, while our social and political systems have not adapted effectively.

For instance, medical technology has increased life spans significantly, yet our pension plans, Medicare, and Social Security have not adjusted, leaving us with enormous funding gaps. Many technologists expect life spans to increase even longer in the future, with average ages over 100 years and many living to as old as 120. How are we going to fund the medical and pension needs of a large group of people for 35 years or longer? Clearly, we need to adapt.

Look also at the work world. A hyper-competitive global environment of accelerated automation is dramatically changing the need for workers and job skills required. Our classical models of government, commerce, and economics are overwhelmed by this situation.

Clearly the technological pace is going to race ahead. Space travel, space mining, and space colonization are becoming feasible. Biotech and bio-genetics will continue to improve health, resist disease, and combat aging. Virtual reality, augmented reality, and artificial intelligence will change how we interact with one another, how we work, and where we work (maybe even whether we work). Drones, driverless vehicles, flying cars, robots, and new currencies will add to the mix.

Here is a short list of some reasons businesses need to adapt:

- Changes in direct competition
  - › More and/or different competitors
  - › Substitution by indirect competitors
  - › Their technology is replacing ours
- Changes in technology
  - › Affecting our behavior, the nature of work, and so much more
- Changes in the economy
  - › Global trade, money flows

- Changes in customers:
  - › Needs and wants
  - › Tastes and styles
  - › Shopping habits
  - › Financial status
  - › Attitudes and beliefs
  - › Demographics
  - › Geography
- Changes in government policy
  - › Monetary and fiscal policy, health care policy, environmental policy, other new regulations
- Changing incentives
  - › Financial and nonfinancial incentives that motivate based on changing workforce priorities and attitudes

How will all these change us? Where we live, what we eat, how we relate, govern, trade / commerce, how long we live, our laws, our global community, our environment, our demographics and psychology. Foresight into these issues is where great opportunity lies.

📊 KEY TAKEAWAYS

- The driving force of foresight is pursuit of the ideal, with a goal to make game-changing, strategic winning moves.
- Foresight requires an open collaborative culture and active ongoing engagement with the market.
- It is not a matter of whether we need to adapt; it's a matter of how and when we will be forced to adapt. However, if we have foresight, we have every opportunity to be first and capitalize on the emerging future.

💡 TRY THIS

Use the table of differences in this chapter as a reminder of the traditional vs. foresight approach, and share it with others so they understand its essence. It helps to have everyone on the same page.

2

Business Is a Continually Emerging Process

T HE PROCESS OF CREATING AND SUSTAINING A BUSINESS CAN BE viewed as a cycle that will either adapt and thrive, or become fatigued and struggle to survive. Our method embodies this cycle:

Discovery leads to *Insight* leads to *Foresight*
leads to *Purpose* leads to *Conduct*

The method begins with Discovery to capture and retain a sense of novelty, adventure, openness, directed observations, and constructive criticism of the status quo. Through Insight we see the major notions, penetrating ideas, patterns, and causes. This leads to Foresight of emerging opportunities and strategic choices. With Purpose we establish our aims, and focus the strength of our efforts. And with Conduct we execute, systematize, and design repetition of our winning formula. Then the process starts over again, with new Discovery leading to Insight and so on.

I begin with Discovery rather than Purpose because leading with purpose limits our perspective to see potentially novel connections we can make to capture opportunity. Having a firmly-defined purpose as a first step can cause myopia, and an unwillingness to change that is counterproductive in today's business environment.

A challenge of the cycle is that we can become locked into the Conduct mode of execution and repetition of the winning formula. When this happens, we become so focused on short-term success that we are afraid to take our eye off the ball. In fact, what can happen is that the active interest of management

Economic progress, in capitalist society, means turmoil.

—Joseph Schumpeter

9

becomes to restrain novelty, curiosity, and openness. Unfortunately, the winning formula, and the team, eventually become fatigued, and lose the will to find a new path forward. We need to continually re-cycle back through the process of refreshing and reinventing the business to secure the long-term future.

Peter Drucker, the noted management consultant and writer, in working with many managements over decades, took the approach of reminding them of the big picture questions and notions they were ignoring. He said that he was more of an "insultant" than a consultant to companies. He didn't tell them what to do; instead, he insulted them, shook them up, and encouraged them to redefine and reinvent their businesses.

The Cycle of Creative Destruction

The need to reinvent and innovate is now more true than ever. Economist Joseph Schumpeter coined the term "creative destruction" back in 1942. He made note of how capitalism both creates and destroys structures, making the old obsolete but also continually creating progress and improving living standards. (As a side note, Schumpeter was concerned that capitalism might be destroyed by its success; that it might create a large intellectual class that would paradoxically make its living by attacking the middle-class values and freedoms necessary for its very existence in the first place. He seemed to have been prescient about this.)

In business, we drive progress through variation and differentiation, and we struggle against competitors, with the market selecting the winners. The cycle also has similarities to evolution as described by Charles Darwin in his book, *On the Origin of Species*. The key components of his theory are Variation, Struggle for Existence (competition is universal), and Natural Selection. These components lead to extinction of some life forms and propagation of the fittest.

A key takeaway is that success does not always breed ongoing success. Rather it can cause a change in behavior that is counterproductive. Knowing that our market is changing as we speak keeps us on our toes - not taking our success for granted.

Example of the Creative Destruction Cycle - Artificial Intelligence

All businesses are going to be affected by artificial intelligence (AI). Creative destruction will occur, perhaps to a degree we have never experienced. Companies that embrace AI will have great opportunity for profit improvement. It will become a competitive advantage used against those that are unwilling or reluctant to change.

We are still in the early stages of AI. It is emerging and there are many potential directions it can take. It is a perfect area for discovery and capture of emerging opportunity through our foresight model. In a recent study on AI by Accenture Research and Frontier Economics, "Why Artificial Intelligence is the Future of Growth," it was stated that AI has the potential to increase economic growth rates more than 4% by 2035 in certain industries (Information and Communication, Manufacturing, and Financial Services), with a weighted average of 1.7% across all industries.[2] There are many other sources you will want to tap to gain foresight about the possibilities for AI and other technologies in your business.

The Dangers of Fatigue

Everything is changing whether we see it or not, and there is a strong tendency for things to gradually come apart when we don't continually improve them. One of the most dangerous times for a business is thus when it is fatigued. This problem is captured in the saying "you can't beat a dead horse." The bestseller *Who Moved My Cheese?* also brought this point home to many.[3] If you are not familiar with the book, it tells the story of two mice who, suddenly, lose their storehouse of cheese that they rely on for food. One of the mice goes about searching for a new source of cheese, while the other mouse does nothing, out of fatigue or laziness, expecting the storehouse to magically return. The former survives, while the latter does not.

In business, you'll see cases of fatigue when companies added new product features that are simply trivial. For instance, companies might simply change the colors or positioning of knobs on products, and call them new and improved. Upgrades in performance are hardly noticeable. New market segments are not to be found. Demand is for replacement purchases, not new installations. Such companies, like the lazy mouse, eventually wither away.

In service companies, customer relationships and the types of services offered can become fatigued. A lack of novelty and almost mechanical interface with customers are typical signs of distress. I have encountered numerous business categories that used to be worth hundreds of millions in revenue that are now near extinction. I'm sure you know similar stories, too.

So, what can be done?

Fatigue makes cowards of us all.

—Vince Lombardi

Innovate for Novelty

Companies faced with fatigue of their products and markets have only two options; they can adapt and change, or they can manage the business with reduced expectations. For those who want to adapt and change, consider this quote from Grant Achatz, one of the most acclaimed chefs in the world, who is especially admired for his creativity in food preparation, presentation, and ambiance of his restaurant, Alinea. To avoid fatigue, he continually innovates:

> People like to think the creative process is romantic. The artist drifts to sleep at night, to be awakened by the subliminal echoes of his or her next brilliant idea. The truth, for me at least, is that creativity is primarily the result of hard work and study.

Achatz is now operating Alinea version 2.0. After ten successful years, he decided to tear his gastronomical wonderland to the ground and start over with a new look and menu. He didn't wait around for fatigue to hit, he beat it to the punch, and got ahead of it. That is true foresight in action. Achatz, like many innovative people, finds that it helps him to visualize his ideas. He has a habit of sketching them on large paper pads.

Breathing new life into an old band, after a decade and a half, Arcade Fire released in 2017 its first No. 1 song on a Billboard chart, "Everything Now." The song was the result of a collaboration with two other musicians, as the band went outside of themselves to look for ideas and new melodies, with great success. This is an example of getting past the "not invented here" bias that often causes problems. We can be reluctant to accept that someone has a better idea than we do. Clearly, in this case Arcade Fire was open to accepting a fresh, novel approach.

Novelty is the primary weapon against fatigue. If the end goal of our method is to arrive at an upward path, novelty is a key component on that path. The most intense experiences of novelty are created by paying exacting attention to detail, delivering enjoyable interactions, and producing effective contrast or differentiation with others. The top restaurants and hotels in the world come to mind here; think of their near fanatical attention to creativity, and the detail of their presentation and service—the use of intense colors, flavors, sounds, aromas, personal engagement, and emotions that affect our sensory experience. We truly enjoy novel products and experiences; they keep us coming back. Consider the detail and differentiation of the original iPhone.

An approach that can be quite successful in driving novelty is *inversion*—considering the opposite of what you want to achieve. Sometimes it is easier to express what you don't want to happen, what you dislike, and what you feel threatened by. For instance, instead of thinking about new approaches to your business, ask, "If I was competing with us, what actions would I take to try to put us out of business?" At a minimum, you will identify vulnerabilities to safeguard against, and ideally you will think of new products and services to offer.

It is important to note that some situations are too fatigued to rejuvenate. Apple faced this many years ago when it was heavily reliant on the computer market and on the verge of failure. Steve Jobs had recently returned to the company to resurrect it. He was asked how he was going to change the company, and he replied (I'm sure tongue in cheek) that he was "waiting for the next big thing." He didn't believe that making a new desktop or laptop computer was the solution. Instead, he was preparing to adapt Apple to a different upward path; which led to the iPod, iPhone, iPad, etc.

Jobs was taking an emergent approach. He wasn't sitting on his hands, though he did have to wait for certain developments to unfold. He had foresight that enabling technology would become available for radically different personal entertainment, camera, computing, and phone devices.

What emerging technologies would make it possible for you to bring valuable new capabilities to your customers?

Two Major Business Mistakes to Avoid

There are plenty of mistakes to be made in business and life. One of the biggest is being in the wrong place at the wrong time. You can assess if you are in the wrong place by comparing your business to others in your industry. For instance, look at your company using the comparisons below:

There was never a good knife made of bad steel.

—Benjamin Franklin

- Commodity vs high-value products or services
- Low cost of selling vs high cost of selling
- Low fixed costs vs high fixed costs
- Low growth vs high growth
- Low profit vs high profit
- Supply vs demand

Is your business going against the grain in your industry? Are you in the right place? For example, if you are selling: commodity-like products through an expensive sales process with high fixed costs in a low growth industry at low profits, and supply is greater than demand, you have the worst of all worlds.

Companies in tough situations like one of these can move to a new area, like Intel did when it moved from cutthroat memory products to microprocessors, or possibly survive by using the "rope-a-dope" principle. It is possible to be the last man standing, as Muhammad Ali was when he coined the term rope-a-dope after defeating George Foreman in 1974. No longer able to float like a butterfly, Ali had adapted, with foresight that he could not beat Foreman by fighting with his high-speed style of the past. He prepared himself to take a lot of punches. He also used physics to his advantage. By laying on the ropes, he transferred much of the impact away from his body. He protected his core, and maintained his ability to retaliate in a timely, powerful way. He delivered a knockout punch to Foreman in the 8th round.

With rope-a-dope, you take punch after punch, intending for the competition to wear down, give up, and exit the business. If you don't have ability to act with energy, speed, or agility, you must have high stamina (significant cash on hand, low cost structure, competitive pricing) to survive.

If you are in a similar situation, you must determine if you can—and want—to do a rope-a-dope to win a war of industry attrition. Can you devise strategies to deflect the punches, outlast the competition, and deliver a timely knockout punch yourself? If you are in a slow-changing industry, the rope-a-dope can still be profitable for some companies for a surprisingly long time. For staple products, for instance, this can go on indefinitely if you have just a small number of competitors remaining on friendly terms, content that you are all surviving in relative peace.

But the goal of our method is to be in the right place at the right time, not to go the rope-a-dope route. I'm not criticizing those who follow that path. I just don't see it as being directed upward; at best, it is forward (status quo), and often it ends up going downward.

Notice I said there are two biggest errors in business. The second one is holding on to a losing situation!

Change Happens by Resolving Conflict

This is obvious when we think of change that occurred in great historical events. The conflict surrounding the changes espoused by Abraham Lincoln and Martin Luther King needs no explanation. Women's rights, gay rights, civil rights, the right to equality under the law, the declaration of independence, the right to vote, the freedom of expression, and so many other "changes" that were unthinkable at one time became realized. Think about how they occurred:

You must be the change you wish to see in the world.

—Mahatma Gandhi

- The change began with constructive criticism of the status quo. This is an obvious source of conflict in and of itself, as many people like the status quo.
- Through insight, the leaders of change identified their major notions and penetrating ideas, as well as the causes of the need for change. They invented slogans to summarize their change: "No taxation without representation," for example, or "We will overcome," or "One person one vote."
- With foresight, they saw the possibilities for a different future and made strategic choices. The need to totally separate from England, for instance, and establish an alliance with France. Women's suffrage commanded the attention of politicians and the public through relentless lobbying, clever publicity stunts, civil disobedience and nonviolent confrontation.
- With purpose, they established their aims and focused the strength of their efforts. The Declaration of Independence, the Constitution, the establishment of the militia, the creation of the treasury and an infrastructure needed to defend the country.
- And with conduct, they executed, systematized, and designed repetition of the winning formula. Establishment of the federal and state government system, which was rolled out to our 50 states. Extension of civil rights law throughout the country.

Obviously change within companies is not as momentous as the political and social examples above. However, it is important to always be aware that any time you try to challenge the status quo, you are going to face headwinds. There will be naysayers. It took time even for Ben Franklin to accept the idea of independence; he was against it at first.

Growing up in Akron, Ohio, I am personally familiar with a big change that one of our companies, Goodyear, developed. The marketing team at Goodyear had foresight that there would be high demand for a new sport performance tire, with branding tied to Goodyear's racing tire program for the Indy and NASCAR circuits. The new tire series, Eagle, became highly successful, but initially it was not received enthusiastically at the highest levels of the company. It required intense commitment and determination from the marketing team to push the program through to completion. Eagle has now been the flagship Goodyear brand for nearly 40 years.

I can attest how difficult it can be to get others onboard, even with issues that seem to be commonsense. It requires patience and persistence. When you are fighting the battle, remember that it is a process. Expect challenges, try to understand their perspective, and take it a step at a time. Listen to them actively, and offer feedback for their concerns so they know you are taking it in (i.e., *"So if I'm hearing you right, you are concerned that if we pursue this opportunity we will take our eye off the ball and miss our sales goal for the year. I understand that would be a concern. The sales goal is important to me, too. It's also important that we not let this opportunity for the future slip away from us. It could be a major boost to the business in two to three years. How about if we…"*). You get the idea.

📊 KEY TAKEAWAYS

- We must be agile, responsive, and adaptable to stay ahead of the cycle of creative destruction. It is riskier not to innovate than to innovate.
- We are in a period where foresight will pay high dividends. Those who capture the waves of artificial intelligence and virtual/augmented reality among other emerging/enabling technologies will have significant advantage.
- You must be persistent and empathetic to cultivate innovation and change in an organization. Don't expect people to easily accept your ideas. It helps to show that you have a method, and that you are purposeful and well intentioned for everyone's benefit.

3

Pathways, Bridges, and "Non-Roads" to the Future

WHEN LOOKING AT NEW POTENTIAL NICHES, SOME MOVES TO adapt are easier to make than others. They may not be as potentially rewarding as other moves, but they can be made without too great an effort. The pathways to new niches include: [4]

The invention of Paris began with a bridge.

—Joan DeJean, Author of How Paris Became Paris

- new customer segments for the same products and services
- new geographies for the same products and services
- new distribution channels for the same products and services
- new features and services for up-market and/or down-market

Beyond these moves, things get considerably more challenging. It becomes not so much making a pathway, but building a bridge. Bridges over, not through, major obstacles require more engineering, resources, and creativity than pathways; however, bridge building can open up enormous new opportunity. Such moves include:

- moving backward or forward in the value creation chain (internal facing or customer facing)
- entering an emerging new space
- creating a new uncontested space

In bridge building, your primary tools are insight about the missing pieces of your strategic puzzle, capital, and people. There is a variety of bridge types that you can use, such as joint ventures, acquisitions of companies and technologies, R&D partnerships, licensing, greenfield projects, alliances, franchising, and outsourcing. One or a combination of these moves might be necessary.

17

Amazon has been a master bridge builder: It has moved both forward and backward in the value creation chain, going heavily into logistics and forward into retail storefront operations; it has moved backward into creation of television show content; it has entered emerging spaces with its cloud services, digital publishing services, etc.; and it is trying to create new space with virtual reality and artificial intelligence among other ventures.

An analogy we can make is the radical transformation that happened to Paris back in the late 1500's and early 1600's, when the walls surrounding the city were removed and bridges over the Seine River were built. Growth of commerce was exponential, which led to a cycle of modernization that made Paris the world's leading city it is today. By the way, the bridges were built by entrepreneurs, not by the government. Entrepreneurial foresight was the spark that started the cycle.

Some personal examples I can offer of pathways and bridges I have helped build include:

- Working for a company with a strong presence in K-12 schools and universities, we did extensive market research on emerging applications of computer-based learning. This led to joint ventures, including one with Apple Computer, to develop branded, differentiated hardware and software.
- For development of a new mass storage product, I coordinated activities with the R&D department of a supplier to develop a magnetic particle capable of ultra-high density recording.
- To jump start sales of a mobile product technology, I coordinated a joint venture that allowed us to sell private branded products while simultaneously designing our own line. This gained significant time to develop sales channels, get customer feedback, get a team in place, etc. so that we were fully ready to launch our own products a year later.

If your future appears to be limited or blocked, think about bridges to new opportunity.

Jumping Off the Evolutionary Path:
The "Non-Road" Approach

As just discussed, you can follow a number of growth paths that are relatively straightforward, or build bridges when needed. But sometimes neither a path nor a bridge leads you where you to need to go. In those times, you may need a "non-road."

Change rooms in your mind for a day.

—Hafiz

Let me explain using this analogy. Think about roads and how they have evolved. In earliest times, they were just trails that were cleared, but over time as needs changed with more traffic and heavier wagons, stones and gravel were added to reinforce roads, then bricks, then asphalt, and now concrete. If we extend this path, the next step would be improved materials, and likely improved processes for paving.

This is fine, but if we consider that roads are becoming increasingly congested, that they are very expensive to build and maintain, and that we are running out of room to add roads in major metro areas, does improving the materials fully meet the needs of today? No. So let's jump off the road and think about whether "non-road" solutions might help us to get from point A to point Z more efficiently. Here are a few ideas:

- use smart video sensor traffic lights to improve flow
- use airborne drones to carry cargo, relieving truck highway traffic
- use hybrid car planes with smart location and collision avoidance control
- use augmented reality systems to reduce the need for in-person meetings
- using driverless technology and artificial intelligence, have apps control the flow of all traffic. This would likely reduce accidents, too, with fewer fatalities, less congestion!
- use 3-D printing capabilities to increase local production of products, reducing need for transport

There are many more ideas you can add here. The key is to think **NON**-road, but to still think of the functions a road fulfills. This is very powerful, so don't minimize it. Try the NON-approach with other areas of interest to you. What jumps do they cause you to make? Use your curiosity and creativity to identify where new opportunities will emerge, keeping in mind the exponential doubling power of technology.

Also, consider related or peripheral opportunities that could emerge, like selling denims and picks and shovels to the Gold Rush prospectors. For example, will drones and other driverless vehicles require new types of filling stations? What kind of maintenance will they require? Will some new type of air control system be needed? Consider the entire eco-system around the product or service.

Here are examples of highly successful NONs, as well as some thought provokers. Some of these are already beginning to jump off the evolutionary path they were on in their field:

- Non-hotel (Airbnb)
- Non-taxi (Uber, Lyft)
- Non-software (software as a service)
- Non-disk drive (Cloud)
- Non-wire (WI-fi)
- Non-bank (crowdfunding)
- Non-paper (eBook and PDF)
- Non-computer
- Non-car
- Non-pen
- Non-phone
- Non-hospital
- Non-doctor
- Non-school
- Non-teacher
- Non-politics
- Non-money
- Non-television
- Non-grocery store
- Non-clothing store
- Non-furniture store

The possibilities are endless!

For categories of interest to you, make a simple table of traits that you expect to emerge soon (see example below).

Category	Next Emerging To	Possibly Jumping Off To
Medical Diagnostics	Clinical databases with natural language query	Smartphone apps with diagnostic measurement
	Video based, remote visits	Artificial intelligence makes the diagnosis with human review
	"Doc in the box" at pharmacies, and other settings	Virtual reality visits

Do you see paths forward in your business? Can you see jumping off points from the evolutionary path? If so, that is a great sign of a vital category. If not, you should consider redefining the category to a point where you can innovate some paths forward. Expand your vision of what is possible in the business to include not just products but activities, behaviors, the removal of walls and obstacles, and new capabilities.

📊 KEY TAKEAWAYS

- Use foresight to explore all seven strategic growth paths.
- Think dynamically, not linearly, about opportunity. Include use of the "non" approach.
- Map the emerging product evolution paths as well as the possible jumping off points to new open space.

Tool: Make tables of evolution and jumping off points for your products. Consider possible "non" versions of your products that could deliver new value and capabilities to customers.

4

Overcoming Bias and Organizational Barriers

Dogma: That which one *thinks* is true, but not necessarily what is true.

Dogma is the box we refer to when we say we need to think outside the box.

Dogma

It's become a cliché to say, "think outside of the box," but I think it's because it has been overused in a way that people do not fully understand. When we say our thoughts are boxed in, we are saying "that's just the way it is" and we are not going to change it. We don't realize the limits we have put on ourselves.

To think effectively outside of the box, you first need to clarify what you hold to be true about a situation, recognizing that your truth may be different from fact. Truth is a concept; it's subjective. Facts are objective. For instance, someone might have a belief that it is an important rule of life to always be positive, and to tune out what they perceive as negative. This is an opinion, not a fact. You could easily counter this belief with evidence of how dangerous it can be to ignore negative information. Sales could be off significantly, yet the positive view will be "this will all blow over, it's just a blip, we'll get it back on track." Clearly this is just an opinion. I've seen many cases where it didn't bounce back, and was a sign of a real problem.

Separating fact from opinion isn't as easy as it sounds. If we have strong biases, fears, pride, incentives, and loyalties, it can be hard to call these out to ourselves. If you want to make a breakthrough you need to do this. Separate the facts of the situation from the subjective, and turn it over and over until you have viewed it from different perspectives.

23

Facts need to be your primary guide, not opinions. You should verify important facts with more than one source if possible. The reason there are fact checkers is that facts can be misstated, taken out of context, exaggerated, not attributed to a true authority or expert. People and companies get in trouble when they put opinions ahead of facts. They can ignore or minimize troubling data trends by glossing them over with positive opinions, not based in fact.

Pride, fear, loyalty, and incentives can make us immune to the hard facts. There are so many examples of companies that ignored the need to adapt. I'm sure you have encountered some, too. Many of our largest corporations in the past 50 years no longer exist; and the list of the Fortune 500 has undergone radical change. As Mark Perry, University of Michigan Professor and Scholar at the American Enterprise Institute, reported on his blog at www.aei.org:

> According to a report released earlier this year by Innosight, based on almost a century's worth of market data, corporations in the S&P 500 Index in 1965 stayed in the index for an average of 33 years. By 1990, average tenure in the S&P 500 had narrowed to 20 years, fell to 18 years in 2012 and is forecast to shrink to 14 years by 2026. At the current churn rate, about half of the S&P 500 firms will be replaced over the next 10 years as we enter "a stretch of accelerating change in which lifespans of big companies are getting shorter than ever" according to Innosight.[5]

Denial is Dangerous

A closely-related phenomenon to dogma is denial. Dogma limits what we accept as being true, whereas denial is the refutation of facts or actual evidence. You have heard of Holocaust deniers and climate change deniers, of course. The world of business is also rife with deniers. These are people who will not accept facts that are unpleasant to them, despite overwhelming factual evidence.

Deniers will take issue with the facts or evidence, saying it is inaccurate, incredible, biased, or even worse, that you are lying. I will go out on a limb here, and say that deniers are very dangerous to the longevity of an organization. The reason I say this is because I have seen deniers destroy companies. The most extreme case of denial I know of was a company president who made it clear to the staff that he did not want to hear of any problems (and there were plenty of problems at this company). He was later fired, but in the meantime a lot of damage was done.

The most damaging forms of denial are:

- Denial that a shift has occurred in the market that puts the current business model at a significant disadvantage.
- Denial that a change in the competitive environment has changed the outlook for sales and profits (i.e., the current plan isn't viable).
- Denial that product quality or product performance is lagging.

For example, deniers may be concerned that negative facts are being used as an excuse for not achieving sales targets. The deniers might realize the facts are true, but they do not want to let the team off the hook for commitments that have been made to the board, stockholders, and Wall Street. Unfortunately, I have never seen a denial situation have a positive outcome. It typically leads to a chain reaction of blame shifting, loss of morale, rumors and gossip, loss of focus, and firings.

When you think you spot denial, the solution is to have a candid, transparent discussion about the validity of the facts and the motivation of the team to address the situation. There is no pleasant or painless way to deal with this; the discussion needs to turn to solutions, and away from distrust, anger, and disappointment. Otherwise, it will spiral out of control.

Notable Evolutionary Losers

It's interesting to note that, in some cases, companies have foresight about emerging changes that could be disruptive to them, yet they do not act to adapt. They are not blindsided, but they are stuck and make poor decisions. For instance, the problem may be that their physical assets (stores, manufacturing plants, etc.), or the physical products they make are facing destruction by a digital business model. They can't unwind their commitments and shift their focus of investment fast enough once the trend has started to really take hold. Once a digital model has taken 20% share from a physical model, it is very hard to recover. It starts a cycle of economic pain and difficulty in attracting top talent to a company. High employee turnover, struggle to find direction, and significant risk of job loss are endemic.

Delay is the deadliest form of denial.

—C. Northcote Parkinson

- **Polaroid**. Had peak sales of $3 billion, and 21,000 employees. Filed bankruptcy in 2001. There is a vestige of the company remaining that manages its intellectual property. Polaroid was a technology leader and had digital products that it could have brought to market, but did not because it could not foresee how it would make a reasonable profit without selling proprietary consumables.

- **Kodak**. Sales peaked at $16 billion in 1996; 2015 sales were $1.8 billion. Could not execute its digital product strategy. It had digital technology, but was reluctant to destroy its cash cow film and chemicals business, so it held back while others overran it.
- **Blockbuster**. In 2004, it had 9,000 stores and employed 60,000. Filed bankruptcy in 2010. Had Netflix on the ropes in 2007, but management infighting lead to a series of new presidents that did not understand the business well, and at one point abandoned the internet streaming model. Netflix had revenue of $8.8 billion in 2016. Apparently, the last president of Blockbuster came from the toy industry, and refused to listen to any of the executive staff.
- **Borders**. Liquidated in 2011 after at one point having 19,500 employees and 1,250 stores. It made a big push into merchandising hard copy products in its stores at a time when the trend to digital media and internet sales hit stride. Its competitor Barnes & Noble has survived, but is not very profitable. B & N did a better job of capturing digital media revenues, selling online, and developing other revenue sources such as in-store cafes.

A culture of innovation avoids dogma and faces denial square on. To avoid dogmatic thinking set aside opinions and ask questions like:

- What would be useful in this situation? What capabilities? What information or data?
- Who might be useful in this situation? Who has a different perspective to consider?
- What if this opinion isn't true? Why doesn't it fit the facts?

If you follow this approach you will at a minimum clarify your thinking, and ideally arrive at novel solutions to break through dogmas that could hold you back.

Opening up to Engagement

One of the basic principles of life is that we affect and are affected. We often lose sight of this, and place undue emphasis on our efforts to affect others. We hear only our own drum, even if we might be missing some beats. This is made worse if we attempt to use our power unilaterally, or to use coercive force. We ignore what the environment is telling us we should be paying attention to, and try to coerce others to listen to our tune.

But when we are in a mode of seeking insight, we need to employ our power to engage, versus our power to control. Being open to persuasion coincides with being able to conceptualize, and envision alternative futures. When hearing an opinion different from yours, it will help if you remember that we discover more by experience than by reason. Put yourself in the mode of an unbiased listener, a keen observer of alternative perspectives. New facts might emerge, helping you gain insights to improve your future course.

We all know that there is a variety of personality types, and that there are personality tests such as the Myers Briggs to help us assess our type. These can help you to be more self-aware of traits that will affect your ability to be open to persuasion. If you find that you have a strong tendency to be judgmental or controlling, you will need to shift yourself into a more receptive mode. I'm not suggesting that you do this all the time, but certainly you do so at times when you are looking for insight about an important issue.

With high value products particularly, effective "selling" is not all about persuading the customer. It is 40% about trust building, and 30% about needs discovery—in other words, being engaged, listening, and asking insightful questions. Only 20% is about presenting solutions, and 10% is about closing.

📊 KEY TAKEAWAYS

- To get foresight you must be open to expanding your perspective. This might be uncomfortable at first, but will pay dividends when you get new insights you never would have gotten otherwise.
- It requires difficult conversations to move people past dogma and denial of facts that are obstructing the business.

- You have to be willing to change business models when yours is no longer working. Of course, this is challenging, but it could be a matter of survival.

☀ TRY THIS

Use these questions to confront an obstructed situation:

- What would be useful in this situation? What capabilities? What information or data?
- Who might be useful in this situation? Who has a different perspective to consider?
- What if this opinion isn't true? Why doesn't it fit the facts?

5

Fostering an Open Culture of Innovation

BEING OPEN HAS IMPORTANT IMPLICATIONS FOR THE INNOVATION of our organizations. I've summarized the contrasts between high and low innovation cultures below:

	High Innovation	Low Innovation
Power	Enabling	Threatening
Conflicting views	Encouraged	Discouraged
Risk taking	Encouraged	Discouraged
Leveling with uncomfortable facts	Encouraged	Discouraged
Problem definition	High input	Low input
Solution finding	Brainstorming	Done in silos
Decision making	Transparent	Opaque

Where on the spectrum does your organization fall? If it is biased toward the right-hand side, what problems do you experience as a result? Is innovation lacking? Is a discouraging culture intentional on the part of management? Perhaps they do not realize that they are stifling input from the organization?

If management is unintentionally discouraging innovation, take steps to shift the balance to a more open dialogue. If it is acting intentionally to discourage innovation, it is possible that a decision has been made to milk the business, simply maintaining operations with little reinvestment.

Remember that change usually comes with conflict, so if you want to make changes, you need to be prepared to work constructively through conflict. Get

Courage is what it takes to stand up and speak; courage is also what it takes to sit down and listen.

—Winston Churchill

people used to your ideas in a non-threatening way, a little at a time. Take time to understand their point of view, and perhaps take a more indirect approach to get on the same page with them. Try to find a way to satisfy both of your objectives.

The next time you are interviewing with, meeting with, or analyzing a company, try to get a feel for where they are on the openness spectrum. Also, determine how intentional the culture is, and whether there is leeway to move it to a more open arrangement.

Organizing for Innovation: A Dual Approach

Every company that has tried to manage mainstream and disruptive businesses within a single organization has failed.

—Clayton Christensen (Harvard professor, author, consultant)

The discussion on this topic centers around using a top-down versus bottom-up organization for innovation. As one example, people compare Amazon's top-down approach to Google's bottom-up approach. I don't think it works exclusively either way. There is usually some of both going on.

The more important distinction is how to best organize for disruptive innovation versus incremental innovation. There should be two innovation engines, one being strongly tied to existing lines of business, and another engine for projects that fall outside the scope of current operations. The reason for this is that the motivations, incentives, and thought processes are very different for projects that are potentially disruptive or alien to the current operation.

Companies with significant resources sometimes establish separate incubator operations with the purpose of pursuing radical innovation, even to the point of housing the incubators in separate facilities or in different parts of the world. They do this because they have learned that it is hard for people to serve two masters that have very different visions, objectives, reward systems, timelines, etc. Merging these two makes it hard to juggle the time and mental energy required, and can create an unproductive tug of war both within individuals and within the company.

Not every company has the resources to set up separate facilities and staff for disruptive innovation. This doesn't mean it can't be done, just that it becomes an even bigger challenge for leadership. In fact, I think this is the most challenging leadership issue of all. When we are innovating within our defined business models, leadership has a very different requirement than when it is shifting to a new paradigm. This is the reason so many companies fail to adapt; the leadership cannot (or will not) transform to a new way of doing business.

I have seen many situations where the writing was on the wall that a market shift was gaining traction and would soon wipe out a product category; for instance, wet chemicals, and certain types of toners and films. These consumable products were very lucrative and company leadership was unwilling to make new products that would cannibalize them. Competitors with new business models walked away with the business.

I've also seen situations where the staff was told "there will be no future unless you get results now, so don't even bother thinking about the next thing." The problem is that the pressure for results never ends. At best in these situations, innovation is done in fits of starting and stopping; it thus loses continuity and effectiveness.

Key innovation leadership requirements are:

- Establishing an effective vision and incentives that align with innovation
  - › For instance, we want 20% of our revenue from new projects in 5 years
  - › We will allocate x% of new project revenue to stock options or profit sharing
- Balancing future needs against pressure for current sales and profit results
- Allocating sufficient resources of money and time
- Organizing productive innovation teams with well-defined objectives
- Driving communication flow, review processes, and recognition of accomplishments
- Maintaining a sense of excitement about the work being done

It helps to set a goal for resource allocation toward innovation. Google is well known to have a high benchmark for this, telling staff that they can use 20% of their time toward any new ideas they want to pursue. This is monitored closely through their objectives and results system, so what everyone is working on is transparent, even in top management.

The amount of resources dedicated to innovation in many tech companies runs 10% to 15%, and in commodity-oriented industries it can be as low as 1% to 2%. The amount you allocate should align with your vision of the next 5 to 10 years, or longer.

You need to be thoughtful about the leadership and organizational requirements of innovation. It will determine the success or failure of the company. Innovation must be intentional and purposeful or it will not happen.

Building Coalitions

Innovation is not a solo activity. If you try to treat it that way, you will fail. You can champion innovation, but in doing so, you must build a coalition of support. I have seen individuals with good ideas fail because they violated this principle.

One of the most memorable failures involved an engineer/product manager who was highly creative, and had breadboarded a prototype video editing system that was way ahead of its time. The problem was that he kept it secret. It wasn't until his unveiling at a special meeting that anyone in the company saw it. As a marketing manager, I could see its potential, but everyone else was blindsided. His supervisor was not pleased he had been kept in the dark. I would have been able to help him explain the market potential for the concept if I had been given time to work with him on it.

I'm sure others could have helped to onboard the concept, too, but his presentation baffled the CEO and other senior execs. The engineer, on the other hand, was baffled why management "didn't get it." His concept might have done very well in the market, but because a coalition was not built around it, it was dead on arrival. Not surprisingly, the engineer left the company shortly after.

We can learn from this example. To effectively champion a concept, we must bring others along on the journey. Ideally there should be early stage support from engineering, product management, marketing, and sales, with some of that being from a senior level. You want to prepare the path (or bridge) for when you are ready to request significant resource allocation. Keeping your coalition involved will greatly improve the cause for your project, and likely pre-sell it so that your funding request will be a mere formality.

Agile Project Management

We want to be highly responsive to change, so it makes sense to use a project management system that allows for rapid iterations. Agile project management has the benefit of being results focused, not process focused; if a direction is not promising it can quickly be put aside to focus on better opportunities.

Contrast this with traditional planning and analysis methods where an unfruitful path might be pursued for weeks.

Agile project management begins with a project vision, and a debriefing release plan that allows for frequent iterations. Formal reviews with top management are scheduled less frequently.

One person should be designated as the project owner. They are the voice of the market.

There also should be a facilitator. The role of the facilitator is to lead the team to higher levels of performance. The facilitator will ensure collaboration, plan and conduct meetings, and guide the team to think of dynamic solutions.

The team members should reflect diverse perspectives, and importantly, must feel passionate about the project. You will want to be wary of putting a process oriented thinker on the team; they might not like the structure of this type of work.

There will be important stakeholders that are not directly involved in the project. It is critical to keep them informed of progress on a regular basis.

Driving Innovation Metrics

These are some questions to help you measure your innovation capacities:

Measure what is measurable, and make measurable what is not so.

—Galileo Galilei

- Does your industry have a winning formula? Gordon Moore of Intel had one for the semiconductor industry that has proven longstanding (since he stated it in 1975). He said that semiconductor capacity would double every two years, so as a competitor in that industry you knew what you had to do to stay in the game from a technology standpoint.
- Do you lead your industry in innovation or are you a follower? Are you a fast follower?
- What is your level of employee turnover? Calculate the ratio of the total number of separations to the average monthly employment for the preceding 12-month period, expressed as a percentage. For example, if the number of separations is 60 and the average monthly employment is 800, then your turnover rate is about 7.5 percent [100 x (60/800)]. You should also separately look at employee turnover by job category and department.
- Employee turnover is a strong indicator of health. It is expensive in many ways, including loss of continuity in customer

relationships. And it is demoralizing to employees to see their co-workers leave for other opportunities. Leading companies have 50% less turnover than average. Industry figures are available from the Bureau of Labor Statistics. Average voluntary turnover across all industries is about 17%.

- What are the economies of scale in your business and industry? Are you able to produce as efficiently, or more efficiently than your competitors?

- Your ability to adapt positively will depend on your innovation, ability to differentiate, and ability to foster strong customer loyalty. You can measure your capability in these areas with surveys of customers; also, you can determine how much your competitors spend on research and development as one measure of your relative investment in innovation.

- You can measure how much word-of-mouth referral business you are getting, and how much churn is going on in your customer base.

- Look at your website inquiries frequency, number of hits, and change over time. Are people becoming more, or less, interested in what you offer?

- Consider the relative strength of your team members. As a rough guide, use a 1-to-10 rating metric for each quality:
  › Ability x Effort x Attitude (Attitude can be -10 to +10); the max score is 1,000.[6]

- Do you have enough people on your team who create opportunities for growth? You might have proficient and competent staff, but at the highest level of performance you also need people who create significant opportunities.

- What is your market share in the niches that you serve? At a minimum, you should target 12%. Deconstruct your market share accordingly:
  1. Estimate the % customers in the niche who are familiar with you and would consider you as a potential supplier. This is your reach, and the % is affected by your advertising, PR, social media, word of mouth, and sales efforts.
  2. Estimate the % fit of your products to the needs of the niche in terms of price, function, reliability and performance.

3. Estimate the % of sales opportunities that you convert into customers. This is affected by the strength of your total offering around the product, as well as by the experience, ambition, and ability of your sales team to engender trust with the customers. Proofs, testimonials, guarantees, and demonstrations can help.

A minimum target I suggest is 80% x 80% x 20% = 12.8%. Serving a niche, you should be able to achieve 80% or better reach to potential customers, and you should have 80% or better product fit to their needs. And lastly, you should be able to close 20% or more of opportunities that come to you. If you don't convert 20% plus, then there is either something missing in your offer or your sales team is coming up short in skills.

One last point here: your biggest leverage point to increase share is your weakest link. By increasing your conversion rate 10 points to 30% you would increase market share to 19%. By contrast you could increase both reach and product fit by 10 points each (while holding conversion at 20%), and share would improve to only 16%.

📊 KEY TAKEAWAYS

- The culture of the company must enable implementation of the foresight method. If it isn't supportive, have serious discussions about the importance of management and the team being on the same page regarding the method and your goals in using it.
- Be careful to sort facts from opinions.
- The effort must be supported with resources and time commitments. Agile management with a team of people good at project thinking (not processes) is ideal for gaining foresight.

💡 TRY THIS

Use the scale of innovation to rate your organization. Ask others to do the same and compare notes in a constructive way, looking for ways to improve. Emphasize that you are on the same team and you want the best for everyone. Calculate your employee turnover and analyze your market share using the formulas in this chapter as indicators of innovation.

PART 2

The 7-Step

Foresight Method

1

Start with Intensive Observation and Discovery

W E ALL HEAR STORIES ABOUT FLASHES OF INSIGHT INTO great new ideas. A flash comes through a connection your mind makes, when you aren't expecting it, making a link using concepts and patterns you have filed away. In other words, your flash comes not from mysterious intervention, but through synapses making neural connections between concepts you have formed, categorized, and sorted. Granted, it is a mystery why it all works though! (After I started working on this book, I happened to look into my personal journal and was surprised; several years ago, I wrote that I prayed for greater foresight. My idea for the book was not a sudden flash, but it did come about in a mysterious way.)

The discovery of patterns and possibilities comes through skilled observation, retention, and reflection in an area of interest to you. Perhaps the best examples of discovery tools are Charles Darwin's "Red," "Transmutation," and "Sketch" notebooks. Darwin collected and recorded vast amounts of information. He made personal observations; exchanged letters; read journals, books, and pamphlets; and made notes of experiments.

Darwin focused intently on naturalist topics, namely botany and biology. In the pre-Google days, this was a slow and tedious process. Just think how much easier we have it with the internet and organizing tools such as Google Keep, Pocket, and Evernote.

We don't want to just acquire lots of facts and data; we want to understand the implications through and through, without bias and intent. This will enable us to create connections and see new patterns of what is possible without being entangled in preconceived notions.

Below are example writings and sketches from Darwin's journals.[7] Notice how he forms questions about his observations, develops hypotheses, cites examples, and notes findings of others. He is truly understanding through and through. This is what we want to do, too.

> Each species changes.
>
> does it progress?
>
> Man gains ideas.
>
> The simplest cannot help—becoming more complicated; & if we look to first origin there must be progress.
>
> If we suppose monads are constantly formed,[8] would they not be pretty similar over whole world under similar climates & as far as world has been uniform at former epoch].
>
> How is this Ehrenberg?[1]
>
> every successive animal is branching upwards,
>
> different types of organization improving as Owen says,[9]
>
> simplest coming in and most perfect and others occasionally dying out; for instance, secondary terebratula may have propagated recent terebratula, but Megatherium nothing.
>
> We may look at Megatherium, armadillos & sloths as all offsprings of some still older type
>
> some of the branches dying out.—
>
> With this tendency to change (& to multiplication when isolated requires deaths of species to keep numbers of forms equable) but is there any reason for supposing numbers of forms equable?—this being due to subdivisions and amount of differences, so forms would be about equally numerous. Changes not result of will of animal, but law of adaptation as much as acid and alkali. Organized beings represent a tree irregularly branched
>
> some branches far more branched—Hence Genera.—)
>
> As many terminal buds dying as new ones generated

Darwin was talented at sketching, and his journals made extensive use of visual representations. He also made many measurements. His notes reference findings of other scientists, clarify his own observations, express doubt or confirmation, develop premises, and ask questions for further investigation.

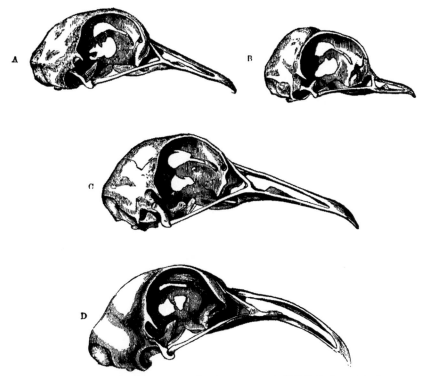

Fig. 24.—Skulls of Pigeons viewed laterally, of natural size. A. Wild Rock-pigeon, *Columba livia*. B. Short-faced Tumbler. C. English Carrier. D. Bagadotten Carrier.

As keen an observer as Darwin was, he was highly impressed by the ability of animal breeders to discern traits. He said that their skill was "one in a thousand" and that they saw many physical traits that he did not. Clearly experience has much to do with this, but also it helps to have a guided observation checklist. Dog judges, for instance, rate a breed on at least 14 criteria.

The lesson for us is that you will get better at observing the more you do it, and it helps to have a sense of what to look for. This feeds on itself, in a cycle of ever-improving skill and insight. Also, it is more important for your propositions (speculations) to be interesting or novel than true; you can validate later. Darwin did not always start with valid premises.

I have no books which tell me much & what they do I cannot apply to what I see... I draw my own conclusions, & most gloriously ridiculous ones they are... The map of the world ceases to be a blank; it becomes a picture full of the most varied and animated figures.[10]

Darwin had a number of theories that he discarded when the evidence disproved them. For instance, isolation of species actually resulted in less variety; he thought from his work at Galapagos that it would be the opposite. Then he had a theory of land bridges that did not hold together totally; some exceptions were too significant to ignore. Some scientists might have ignored the exceptions and made the data fit, but he had a higher motive. He finally arrived at a theory of cross-breeding of varieties and inbreeding to make new varieties that became his foundation for explaining the mechanism of evolutionary adaptation.

Another great "journaler" we can learn from was Leonardo da Vinci. He maintained extensive journals on about 50 topics ranging from philosophy, flight, astronomy, anatomy, war machines, music, botany, hydraulics, optics, and acoustics. Here are examples of his architectural thoughts about walls, and his famous visualization of the human form, the Vitruvian Man (on next page) from one of his journals.

On Fissures In Walls

First write the treatise on the causes of the giving way of walls and then, separately, treat of the remedies.

Parallel fissures constantly occur in buildings which are erected on a hill side, when the hill is composed of stratified rocks with an oblique stratification, because water and other moisture often penetrates these oblique seams carrying in greasy and slippery soil; and as the strata are not continuous down to the bottom of the valley, the rocks slide in the direction of the slope, and the motion does not cease till they have reached the bottom of the valley, carrying with them, as though in a boat, that portion of the building which is separated by them from the rest. The remedy for this is always to build thick piers under the wall which is slipping, with arches from one to another, and with a good scarp and let the piers have a firm foundation in the strata so that they may not break away from them.

In order to find the solid part of these strata, it is necessary to make a shaft at the foot of the wall of great depth through the strata; and in this shaft, on the side from which the hill slopes, smooth and flatten a space one palm wide from the top to the bottom; and after some time this smooth portion made on the side of the shaft, will show plainly which part of the hill is moving.[11]

The journals of Darwin and da Vinci have been published and are freely viewable online. You can get a good feeling for the types of observations they made, and read about the development of their thought processes.

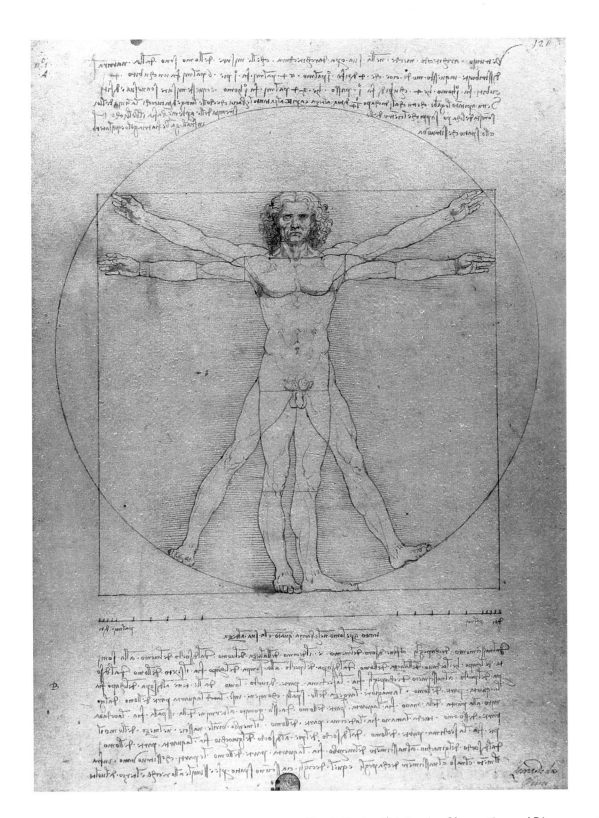

Observing and the Value of Notetaking

You can start your voyage of discovery by observing and writing observations in a notebook like Darwin and da Vinci. Why not give your notebook a name? Darwin called one of his The Transmutation notebook. The observations you write, diagram, graph, and sketch will provoke new connections in your mind of opportunities to explore. Capture those new ideas immediately, before they fly away. These ideas don't always come as eureka moments. In fact, two main differences of entrepreneurs from others is that they tend to be more curious, but more importantly they don't disregard the little things that are seen every day by millions of people and ignored.

Four general categories are helpful to observe in business—economic, social, political, and technological. Within those four categories, note your observations of the following:

- Behavioral influences: outlooks, incentives (profits, etc.), demands, problems, beliefs, attitudes
- Structural powers and centers of influence: individuals, groups, companies, governments, countries

As you make your notes, keep in mind that the most valuable insights are those that question the status quo, identify patterns, and make analogies to different fields. For instance, note patterns of cause and effect, or patterns of behavior. Notice how one field of interest is similar to another field. When you encounter a problem and think, "there must be a better way," write it down and draw a sketch of it. Then—and this is critical—redesign the pattern to create a new version.

Here's a simple example. Say you notice that it is time consuming and expensive to send reps to a site to give free estimates for your service. The time it takes limits your ability to quote more business. You read that a company in Australia has made huge gains in sales of lawn care services with little addition to staff by using Google Maps to view sites and provide quotes the same day. Low cost, no delay, more quotes, more business. Put these insights together and you have a new idea.

The method described in this book is flexible in that there can be several "jumping-in" points. You don't need to come at it by looking at ideas in sequence; possibilities reside in connections that aren't always logical or chronological. At some point, you need to develop a working hypothesis or premise to test, but you need not start there.

High-Tech Journaling Tools

Keeping a hard copy notebook is a good way to capture your observations and thoughts. Many great leaders across all disciplines have used hard copy journals. In your work today, however, you may be likely to find much of your information through the internet, and capturing that can be expedited through several free or low-cost easy-to-use tools.

The most basic web clipping tools I use are Pocket and Google Keep. These apps work with your browser to quickly capture links to web pages of interest. You can tag the links with notations, manage them in folders, and perform search functions within the applications. This makes it easy to refer to content you have saved and sort through it using your tags and folder designations. Pocket offers suggestions for additional content you might be interested in. Google Keep has the advantage of letting you add and organize your own notes, not just web content.

A capability that these apps do not offer that might come in handy is to do keyword searches within the body of the content you have saved. Pocket and Keep can search titles and tags, but if, for example, you want to search all your saved content for the keyword "virtual reality", these apps will only point you to content that you have tagged "virtual reality" or has" virtual reality" in the title.

Microsoft OneNote and Evernote have the capability to do keyword search through all your saved content, regardless of tags. In our example, they will highlight all the instances of the occurrence of "virtual reality" throughout your saved content, even if you did not tag it. In one article, you might find it highlighted 5 times, and in another article 8 times. OneNote and Evernote also provide additional organizing benefits you might find useful, so it is worth looking at them closely. They give you more flexibility to reorganize and re-sort your content than Pocket or Keep.

You can also keep your journal notes in OneNote and Evernote and search them. You can search notes you retain in Keep as well. Whichever route you go, you will be glad to have the information readily available when you need it.

I keep six honest serving men, they taught me all I knew. Their names are What, and Why, and When and How, and Where, and Who.

—Rudyard Kipling

📊 KEY TAKEAWAYS

- Your goal with discovery is to observe and make note of a wide variety of inputs, keeping an open mind and not pre-judging. The types of inputs will be discussed in more detail in the next chapter. You will want to prepare a discovery plan for your team, with assignments of activities.

- You don't want to just acquire lots of facts and data; you want to understand the implications through and through to question the status quo, create connections, and see new patterns of what is possible.

- Think ahead to when you will want to sort and analyze your discovery information! Given that need, tag your information for referencing. It helps to identify the type of information you are entering into the journal, for instance, making notations such as: topic; new idea; opinion; observation; fact; action item; and red flag.

☼ TRY THIS

Use the high-tech journaling tools, but also make use of written notes and sketch your concepts, too. Anything that will help to embed them in your mind for later use.

Scout the "Market Terrain"

T O SET THE STAGE FOR COMPETITIVE ADVANTAGE, IT'S IMPORTANT to have a good understanding of your market terrain—the behavioral and structural influences acting on your customers (or your end-users), competitors, resellers, and suppliers. In terms of behaviors, the following areas are useful to stay abreast of the following: outlook, incentives (profits, goals), demands, problems, beliefs, and attitudes. In terms of structural influences, they can be categorized as: individuals, groups, companies, industries (niches), governments, and countries.

When analyzing customer and competitor behaviors, here are aspects to pay attention to:

- Is the outlook on them highly optimistic or cautious? Are they expanding capacity, adding employees, and setting aggressive goals? Do they have objectives for innovation, or upgrading of their capabilities?

- In terms of attitude, are they calculated risk takers or conservatives? Leaders or followers? Big thinking or small thinking? Global thinking or localized thinking? Aggressive or complacent?

- What are their beliefs and values? How important to them would you estimate are the following: integrity, respect, loyalty, family, knowledge, reliability, efficiency, creativity, diversity, ecological and societal responsibility, openness, fun, and adventure?

- Look at the ties between customer problems, demands, and incentives. To increase sales and profits, what performance is being demanded of sales, marketing, and operations? What problems will they encounter, and how incentivized are they

Mr. Disney and his staff were constantly scouting for great stories to bring to life on film.

—Annette Funicello

to succeed? How might you help them to increase speed and quality of execution, and make them secure in their decision to work with you?

By examining these issues, you will get a clearer sense of the lay of the land, and how the actors are intending to change it in the future. For instance, there can be a radical shift in demand for a product—call it a tipping point—where you might discover that even the most stalwart long-term customers intend to change horses to a new technology. Similarly, through these questions, you might identify when a new product or technology is going to hit an inflection point where demand is going to skyrocket.

For instance, while working with one company, I found that there was little demand for products from a European maker of rugged mobile computers in the larger warehousing and logistics markets, but there was significant opportunity for them in mining, agriculture, marine, forestry, construction, oil services, and flight services. These markets had a very different terrain than the usual ones—with different needs, competitors, attitudes, etc. This insight helped the company to make a successful change in strategy.

In addition to specific customer and industry trends, it is useful to assess how general economic, social, political, and technological trends might affect your market terrains.

Your possible moves may also be affected by your industry structure. It can be diverse and fragmented, or it can be highly concentrated in the hands of a few goliaths. It is rarely successful for a small firm to compete directly against a goliath, and it can be difficult for a small firm to sell to a goliath customer. I once consulted with a firm that wanted to make a big push to sell electronic components into the medical devices industry; however, that industry is largely controlled by a few players, including Medtronic, who have extremely rigid vendor qualification criteria. Selling to them was going to be a huge undertaking, and the volumes of the smaller medical device suppliers were not high enough to warrant special interest. That initiative was tabled for future consideration so that other industries with lower barriers could be pursued.

A general power law that often applies to business is the 80/20 rule, with 80% of the demand coming from only 20% of the customers. It is always useful for planning to determine if your market terrain follows a power law such as 80/20, or perhaps 90/10 or 70/30. Some are even more diverse, following a 1/n pattern, where n is your industry rank; e.g., the #2 ranked firm is ½ the size of the largest firm, #3 is ⅓ the size of the largest and so on down the line. There are variations of these power laws, so take time to discover how they affect your industry.

Identify centers of influence in the niches you serve or want to serve. These could be lead users who set the pace in their industry, or user evangelists who can influence and refer 10 or more new customers to you. Talk with consultants, resellers, research analysts, stock analysts, journalists, editors, and sales reps. Trade insights with them.

Pay Attention to What Everyone Is Whining About

I agree with the quote here from Juliette Gordon Low. The best insights I have ever gotten came from scouting missions in the field.

Scouting rises within you and inspires you to put forth your best.

—Juliette Gordon Low

Mark Cuban said it's a good idea to make special note of what we are whining about, for the simple reason that it could mean there is a product or service idea buried in there. If you are unhappy about something, it's possible that others are, too, and that everyone would welcome a solution.

If you stop to think about it, many of our popular products and services came from people who were upset about a problem or had a bad experience and wanted to change it. Have a problem with taxis, start a ridesharing service. Have trouble meeting people on campus, start a social network. Don't like the web browsers available, start a new one. Think office space is too expensive, start a shared office service. See that hotels sell out when big events come to town and there is no place to stay, offer a home rental service.

What are your customers whining about lately? The experience of your customers is a goldmine of potential ideas for new features and new products. It is important, and easy, to capture information from your customer-facing employees about complaints and requests your customers tell them. You should also proactively search for customer feedback via surveys and field visits. It can be an eye-opening experience to see firsthand how your customers are using your product! I have found situations where customers improvised (rigged together) new "accessories" that they used with a product. We used this insight to design new features and accessories to better meet their needs. You can also get good ideas from users on the front line who operate your products on a day to day basis. They can tell you about ways the product could be made better for their situation.

Importance of Technology in Driving Behavior

Behavior is affected by many factors described by leading psychologists such as Jung, Freud, James, and others. But a factor not often considered is technology. Our behaviors are in a cycle of both affecting and being affected by technology. Since early civilization, the creation of new technological tools for farming, hunting, building cities, manufacturing, communicating, computing, and interacting have shaped us—and we in turn have shaped new technologies.

When analyzing your customers' behaviors, pay attention to the influence of technology in their lives at work and home. Look at how they use technology to interact with others, how involved with social media they are, the types and brands of devices they use, the types of apps and software they find most useful (and those that they don't), what they like and dislike about technology in their lives. Ask yourself what would they like to do but can't because they are feeling limited? From these insights, you will have a clearer picture of how to engage with and relate to your customers, and how you might help them with the limitations they feel.

Consider how technology and behavior are interacting to affect Comcast and ESPN. Increasingly people are cutting the cord to cable TV because of all the new streaming options, yet Comcast has continued to do well by offsetting this loss with growth of its high-speed internet service, and bundling it with phone and cable TV packages. ESPN, on the other hand, has seen significant decline in subscriptions (cutting the cord), which to date it has been able to offset with price increases. Some analysts believe that ESPN is going to slowly evaporate if it continues on this track though. Eventually the price increases will become too painful for customers, and ESPN will need to adapt or fade away, especially if Amazon, Netflix or Facebook start bidding for pro sports media rights.

Technology has both threatening and enabling aspects. While we have the benefit of being highly interconnected, some of us have friends who lost their jobs because they were replaced by automation. It started in factories but is reaching increasingly into offices. I know PhDs in the field of market research who have been replaced by artificial intelligence software.

Technology was intertwined in a major way in the election of Donald Trump as president, as it was in the election of Barack Obama before him. Social media, tweeting, fake news, internet trolls, email hacking, and rust belt resentment of lost factory jobs demonstrates the momentous impact of technology on behavior.

The Importance of Incentives in Driving Behaviors

Incentives are key to driving both negative and positive behaviors. Typically, we think of money as the main incentive that drives people. However, monetary incentives can cause performance to suffer in ways that undermine customer experience, such as undue selling pressure. They can also cause misstatements of financial performance, cheating, collusion, conflict of interest, and "playing the system." When designing incentives, it is critical to consider all the behaviors that could be influenced, not just the intended behaviors. If there is a crack or loophole, it will surely be abused.

Consider also that many younger workers today are not as motivated by direct compensation as in the past. New indirect incentives such as flex-time hours, paid maternal and paternal leave, and company subsidized lunches, education, transportation, and housing are becoming more common. Google, for instance, offers most of these benefits.

Thoroughly consider which employee incentives will help your customers. Determine how their compensation is tied to: sales, profits, productivity, retention, customer satisfaction, new product development, quality, return on investment, etc. Then be their partner in helping them to achieve their goals and incentives. Build this insight into your offering and your customer communications. More on this later in the section about "creating stickiness."

Identifying Useful Patterns

The most useful types of patterns to recognize in business are:

Creativity involves breaking out of established patterns in order to look at things in a different way.

—Edward de Bono

- Similarities, i.e., analogies—this is like that
- If-then, i.e., cause and effect
- Effective contrast, i.e., standing out meaningfully in a crowd
- Skewed patterns, i.e., getting unexpected exponential results

Analogies are helpful when you can see a concept in one area that could be used effectively in another; such as seeing how a business practice at Google could be useful in a manufacturing company.

The value of understanding if-then is self-explanatory. It is always helpful, though deceptively difficult, to determine cause and effect in complex systems, but it can lead to a winning formula with large payoffs.

Effective contrast, also called effective differentiation, is important to avoid a commodity mentality. The differentiation you offer must be truly meaningful and of value to customers. Difference just for difference's sake is not useful. Also, empty "We statements," such as "We are the leader," and "We are #1" should be avoided. Look at your website and marketing materials critically for "we statements." If your first impression message is more about you than about the customer and how they can benefit from your offering, work on changing the balance. Make sure that you associate your features with benefits; lead with the benefits, then support them with feature specifications.

When you see a skewed pattern, one that has exponential results, you've found a potential gold mine of a niche. Dig in to learn everything you can about it, and do all you can to protect, defend, and leverage it.

Identifying Disruptive Traits

All fixed set patterns are incapable of adaptability or pliability. The truth is outside of all fixed patterns.

—Bruce Lee

The concept of a disruptive trait is one based on exaggeration that splits the market into those with the trait and those without it. It's a form of strong differentiation.

When selecting traits to exaggerate, it's important to distinguish between product-level design and business-level design.

For products, it's most helpful to look at functional needs, including related hard and soft areas around the primary function. For example, consider a product's core essence—at what point is a car no longer a car or a pen no longer a pen? There must be a "coreness" to a product. Beyond the core, everything else around it can be modified and adapted to special market needs, including soft areas such as image. Clearly, both cars and pens have markets for status image, as well as markets for functional differentiation in performance, size, value, etc. And the related functionality can sometimes be extended when you consider the environment the product or service is used in. For instance, printers now often include a scanner, phones have cameras, and some handheld computers have barcode scanners.

For business-level design and trait selection, the key question is, "How is the customer changing?" Priority analysis is what you want to get at here. Where are your customers trying to go, and what are the sticking points in achieving their goals? Help solve the sticking points in their business and you will go far to gaining their loyalty. Later in the book there is a section on Creating Customer Stickiness that has suggestions on how to offer unique value to your customers.

Identifying Relatively Stable Traits

We have been emphasizing change; however, there are aspects of many businesses that are relatively stable and do not need modification. For instance, there will always be needs for: entertainment, nourishment, knowledge, information, infrastructure, medical care, housing, human interaction, connection, communication, transportation, wealth management, logistics, energy, and many other fundamental global requirements. And there will always be demand for higher productivity and efficiency, lower costs, safety, variety, convenience, simplification, sensory appeal, status, integration, access, wellness, and design aesthetics.

The extent to which you can define your markets and your competencies around fundamental customer wants, needs, and problems will help to determine the stability of your business platform. If you narrowly define your opportunity around a type of product, your future is more susceptible to disruption.

An example of a relatively unstable platform is defining your business in terms of a function. To say you are a retailer has clearly become problematical in recent times. In fact, many intermediary, broker, and trader business models have been upended. Companies that identified themselves primarily as manufacturers have gone through pains. Recall our discussion of Polaroid and Kodak. How might they have responded better to the market if they had identified their platform as enabling widespread sharing of images to improve human connection, as opposed to making cameras and selling film (the film being by far their main interest)? Perhaps they would have devised a new business model like Instagram or Facebook, and be thriving today. Consider your business platform. Do you define your business broadly enough to allow for freedom to maneuver and adapt to changing competition and market demands?

This same principle applies to jobs as well. Jobs that have a narrowly defined function are more susceptible to replacement: cashier, driver, assembly worker, bank teller, insurance claims representative, journalist, pilot, and financial analyst, for instance. Are you preparing your employees for flexible jobs?

📊 KEY TAKEAWAYS

- Make a scouting plan with your team, defining the information you want to capture and the methods you will use to obtain it. Identify key people you will interview, secondary research sources you will tap, and information you might purchase. Consider: books, magazines, associations, industry analysts, conferences, trade shows, seminars, annual reports, customer surveys, competitor strengths and weaknesses, and surveys of lost customers.

- Remember that foresight comes from active engagement, so spend significant time outside the office interfacing with people. Especially spend time with those you know to be innovative in their own right.

- Pay attention to what people are whining about. Where there is pain there is also opportunity for improvement.

3

Define Venturesome Ideas

U P TO THIS POINT WE HAVE BEEN ACTIVELY OBSERVING AND SCOUTing the market terrain. Now it is time to make full use of the data, facts, and insights to define possible new venture concepts and projects.

Sorting Your Observations and Premises

Sorting and categorizing your observations is one of the most valuable talents you can have. There are dozens of themes you can sort on, and it helps to use a wide assortment of them so that you can get a sense of which ones are most insightful about the workings of the market you are analyzing.

He who can properly define and divide is to be considered a god.

—Plato

What you are trying to get at are the X factors—those variables that have the most significant impact on the outcome, such as the greatest impact on sales in your various market segments. You will likely find that different market segments have different X factors.

When you sort market information you will want to consider:

- Customers by industry type
- Buying criteria of customer types: factual and attitudinal by rank in importance
- Sales cycle: how long to close, frequency of purchase, life cycle, size of purchase
- Buying influences by title
- Market concentrations of customers: 80/20, etc.
- ROI payback criteria demanded by customers
- Sales channels to reach various customer types (direct versus indirect)

- Product segments in terms of price performance
- Competitor share and positioning by market segment
- Growth of segments in profits and revenues
- Unavailable market—no fit with your products or is captured by competitors with no opportunity for you to influence
- Other criteria you want to consider based on your discovery observations.

When you have organized your thoughts, give a debriefing to your organization. You can say, "I've been actively looking into the opportunity of XYZ, and here are interesting observations I've made to date." You might want to make it an interactive, semi-structured, or even a workshop type-presentation with props or other show-and-tell support tools. The end goal of the debriefing is to identify opportunities for further investigation or assessment using your entire team's input.

Example: Sorting Facts and Data About the Emerging Future of Pro Football

This is an overview of how you might sort observations and thoughts if you were involved in the business of the NFL, and use them to predict its future and prepare for changes. These aren't answers; they are simply speculations and observations for further discussion and investigation.

As mentioned, let's make use of notes of outlooks, incentives, demands, problems, technologies, beliefs and attitudes, all from the perspectives of the key powers and influencers of the NFL. Also, we want to examine the competitive entertainment activities that consumers can choose. In practice, you might have many pages of notes on these topics, such as extensive data on cable cutting, the move to streaming video, and possible new revenue models. Also, there are attitudinal and demographic changes emerging that you would want to cover in depth. You would have notebooks full of discovery observations for a business as large and complicated as the NFL. For now, though, I've included just brief notes.

General viewership and attendance

- Game attendance flat since 2008 with uptick in 2016.
- TV ratings down 8% in 2016, possibly due to election.
- NFL seems to be at or near saturation. Fatigue is showing. Still hugely popular but there is audience churn going on.

- Collegiate football is gaining audience.

Economics of the business

Here we would comment on notable and significant changes going on with:

- Cost trends
- Changes in revenue mix of merchandise sales, ads/network revenues, ticket sales, concessions sales

New revenue models

- How is cable cutting impacting our viewing audience?
- Streaming live versus on demand. People like to watch football live, not delayed. How can football make the streaming model work better in real time? Idea. Can we bundle services with Amazon or Netflix?
- ESPN can stream, but is losing share
- Can we get better statistics on mobile viewing of games?
- College football is embracing streaming and having success with it. Almost 16 million unique streams were made in the 2016 season, up 17% from 2015. What can we learn from them?
- Music industry comparison—Music business was dead, but now in resurgence. There are new business models for ads, streaming, singles, new combos; the innovators are winning, offering quality, convenience, mobile, bundles free with ads or paid. What can we learn here? Music went through 10+ years of hardship before waking up to new reality.

New venues

- Video gaming venues are evolving
- There are new "stadiums" in the US, London, and Asia for competitive video gamers
- Idea. With virtual reality/ augmented reality, we could possibly have a new e-venue for football. People could attend every game "live" if they wanted to. Example; Dallas could have a separate e-venue stadium where home crowd could go to watch when the Cowboys are playing away, would have the look and feel of a live stadium game. Perhaps other events could be piped in as well: bands, baseball, basketball, etc.

- Idea: we should meet with e-venue owners

Scheduling

- There are complaints of oversaturation of NFL football. It is on weekdays and weekends. There is a longer schedule with more games. The schedule has grown over the years from 10 games, to 12 games, to 14 games to now 16 games.
- Complaints that games are too long, too many commercials
- How can we test impact of scheduling on viewership and attendance? Would less equal more? Make it more of a special event?

New technology

- The NBA has been meeting with virtual reality companies. Need to find out more about what they are thinking here. Perhaps we can collaborate with them?
- Magic Leap will be introducing augmented reality that might be appropriate for arena settings. We need to meet with them.

New demands of the audience

- We are seeing less involvement at the high school and PeeWee level. Peaked in '08, '09 been in slow decline ever since. Youth football participation in the South is increasing somewhat, declining in the Midwest. What can we learn from this difference in participation?
- Can we think of new ways to interact with the fans?
- According to Statista there has been steady growth in hiking, biking, camping, and other participatory experience activities
- Millennials not as interested in football or other organized sports.

Special Issues

- Attitudes—there is concern about concussions, safety of the game. This has centered heavily on the NFL, poor publicity. Need to take stronger action to protect players from brain damage.
- Recent reports state that research has found widespread early brain damage in younger players.

- We already behind on this issue. We need to put a priority on rules changes and new technology to protect player safety.

International reach

- Should we set up a greenfield project in England—London or Manchester? Idea. Have a London-based team that we would back for at least 10 years to gain traction. Would play in the US and in London. Could possibly be an entré to establish other European teams.
- Other countries of interest in Asia? How about Australia and New Zealand?

Demographics

- The demographic of the NFL fan is skewing older. In the past 10 years, average age of viewership has gone from 46 to near 50. Viewers in the 18-24 age segment are declining.
- South versus Midwest trends in youth leagues, high school, college. Why the differences in interest in football?

Competitive entertainment

- Competition with college football. College football attendance and ratings remain very strong and growing.
- Soccer youth participation in the US is up 11%. What does that mean for us?

As you can see from this simple sorting, there are many emerging issues the NFL must discuss, collaborate with others on, and test. Much is outside its normal purview. They need to look at how the customer is changing, player safety, as well as delivery of the entertainment product itself.

When you initially sort your facts and data, call out action items for further discussion, research, and testing. Speculate about possible connections and patterns you see. Comment on other resources of enabling information you will want to tap. The goal of this is to bring fresh thinking, find critical insights, and expand the map of new opportunities. Don't throw away ideas at this point, even if they seem crazy. At the end of this process you want your team to come away with a list of potential projects, product concepts, and venture ideas you will rate and rank for priority action using a technique discussed in the next chapter.

Connecting Your Ideas - Thinking Nonlinear

Linear thinking most often results in incremental change, like doing something faster or making it bigger or smaller. Examples: Supersize me, hurry in for even deeper discounts, get your rental faster than ever, here's the new and improved Tide, introducing spicier wings, and so on. Incremental innovation reaches limits to where it becomes dull and ho-hum, generating a "so what" reaction.

Consider the NFL situation in losing audience share discussed earlier. Linear thinking will not solve their problem. Simply offering more games per season, a few new rules, new special effects, or different broadcasters will not fix the loss of audience. These ideas have already been tried. They need to think more dynamically, or nonlinearly. It begins by putting aside the football lens and putting on a wider focus "entertainment" lens—looking at the trends, behaviors, technologies, and demographics of many other global entertainment venues.

People take the longest possible paths, digress to numerous dead ends, and make all kinds of mistakes. Then historians come along and write summaries of this messy, nonlinear process and make it appear like a simple, straight line.

—Dean Kamen

Golf is a game I have enjoyed since I was in grade school, but unfortunately, it is in decline. Rounds of golf are down significantly, there are fewer golf courses, and the costs per round continue to increase. However, Top Golf is thriving. Top Golf is an entertainment venue, a souped-up driving range so to speak, with games for all, food, drinks, and technology. It even appeals to non-golfers. Golf has tried to speed up the game and make other changes to no avail. In other words, linear thinking is hurting golf, while a nonlinear approach of golf as an entertainment venue is working well for Top Golf.

An acquaintance of mine invested in several frozen yogurt franchises as a sideline. At first things went well, but soon competitive yogurt stores opened near his locations, dampening his enthusiasm. He had many challenges staffing the stores with employee turnover, theft, and absenteeism. He has now gotten rid of the stores. Contrast this with FroYo, the self-serve, robotic, 24/7 yogurt franchise. The FroYo people obviously listened to the market, and designed a new business model to capitalize on robotic capability and people's willingness to use self-services. They asked, what would a non-store yogurt business look like?

The key to progress is to discover and capture new knowledge.

Knowledge is interdisciplinary, so it pays to stay informed of different disciplines that can affect your work, such as economic, political, international, demographic, and technological disciplines. These can change over time as markets converge, and new trends and technologies emerge.

Recognize also the importance of social and behavioral trends, no matter your industry. After all, your customers and their businesses are affected by intangible factors of a social and behavioral sort, too. Take advantage of the free tools available, such as Flipboard, to get specific/topical news feeds of articles from sources like the MIT Technology Review, Wired, Popular Science, The Economist, Fast Company, and many other excellent publications. Use the widest lens you can use to spur innovation in your business.

Transforming Activities and Objects

The digital transformation of activities has grown incredibly over the past 20 years. Think of all the activities that have changed, or are going to change soon: finding a date, reading a book, banking, communicating, paying, shopping, driving, taking a taxi, booking a flight, designing a product, going to school, diagnosing a patient, typing, watching television, and more. When you look at where the real growth has been in the tech sector, services totally dominate with companies like Google, Amazon, Facebook, Airbnb, various cloud service companies, and many others.

We always plan too much and always think too little.

—Joseph Schumpeter

Meanwhile, Apple has made a huge impact with the digital transformation of many physical products. The making of objects is being advanced primarily by making them smarter. Increasingly, objects are becoming capable of communication and control within the Internet of Things. Climate controls, jet engines, vehicles, warehouses, factory equipment, home security systems, and many other devices are incorporating sensors and actuators that allow for control through the internet.

Manufacturing has seen dramatic loss of employment over the last 20 years, though it remains at a relatively constant 12% of GDP in the US. The use of automation allows higher manufacturing output with fewer employees. Also, the use of third-party contract assembly services has shifted jobs out of the manufacturing sector.

If we were to compare these two categories of change, however, in general, we will find that the biggest opportunities looking ahead are in transforming services, more than in transforming objects. In the report from Accenture mentioned in the first chapter, they foresee that service industries are going to go through a major change in the next decades due to new technologies and especially artificial intelligence. Virtual/augmented reality will have a large impact as well.

The graph below shows how growth of employment in services far surpasses employment in manufacturing from 1940 to 2011, and this same trend is predicted to continue into the next 20 years. This makes sense when you consider how much larger the service sector is than the manufacturing sector. For example, the opportunities emerging to transform education and medical services alone are enormous

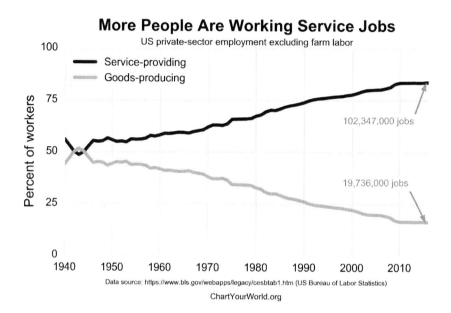

More People Are Working Service Jobs
US private-sector employment excluding farm labor

Data source: https://www.bls.gov/webapps/legacy/cesbtab1.htm (US Bureau of Labor Statistics)

ChartYourWorld.org

Ways to Get Effective Input from Others

Along with debriefing the organization about your innovation projects, there are numerous techniques you can use to gather input from others and generate discussion.

Envisioning sessions: This type of session aims to examine the 5- to 10-year outlook for your business and industry. The framework of discussion can follow the Model of Adaptation (which we will discuss in a later chapter) where you consider how to adapt to scenarios you foresee.

In these sessions, you will want to zoom out before zooming in to look at the wider view of your markets and competitive situation. Also, discuss how you expect your competitors to adapt (perhaps they have even made public statements about this). Note that it is important not to let any individual dominate or bias the discussion. It can also be useful to have breakout groups, in which you ask for written comments on the various topics to ensure that everyone's input is included.

In my experience, there can be widely disparate views expressed in these sessions, and the differences will not get resolved during them. Make it clear that the goal is simply to get the differences out on the table, not to be taken as right or wrong, but as possibilities to evaluate in ongoing discussions.

Round tables: These sessions are great to bring in an expert who can expose your team to perspectives on a new topic of interest. Consider having a half-day session along with a meal and time to mingle with the expert. Have a guided agenda, but also allow for some spontaneity.

Discussion groups: Establish a regular group to discuss over lunch or coffee new innovation projects. Include different disciplines from engineering, marketing, sales, service, etc. Talk about news updates, problems and obstacles, possible solutions, or brainstorm a topic (e.g., let's come up with 20 ideas to improve the quality of our internet-based customer service).

Councils: Sponsor a council of customers or resellers that you interact with on a regular basis, say every six months. This can be a good vehicle to keep you engaged with a view from the marketplace.

Others: There are also seminars, trade shows/conventions, industry analysts, journalists and editors, focus groups, and executive field interviews.

Remember, foresight comes from being active in the flow of things—observing, discussing, researching, prototyping, hypothesizing, finding patterns, making notes, sketching ideas, experimenting, and testing. Look at gaining foresight as an ongoing journey.

Clarifying Your Major Notions and Penetrating Ideas

I like to be right. I try not to miss the big ideas, forget the little ones, and try to get them right.

—Jeremy Grantham, chief strategist of GMO, one of the world's largest asset managers

Earlier I stated that through insight we see the major notions. Here is what I mean by that. Consider Andrew Carnegie, the steel magnate of the late 1800s. He knew through his connections and experience that there would be a significant expansion of the railroad network in the U.S., and therefore that there would be a need for the raw materials to build it. He capitalized on a new technology to make steel more efficiently before anyone else saw the potential, and became one of the wealthiest Americans of all time.

This is the format for writing down your major notion:

This _____ (situation, problem, or incapability)
makes this _____ (notion) necessary or possible.

First start with the need or potential demand, then determine the possible solutions. Don't do the reverse (have a solution and go looking for problems), otherwise you will be like the proverbial hammer looking for a nail. For instance, don't say I have this possibility to make a virtual reality system, I wonder who needs it? Instead, find a situation in need of a solution, and tailor your notion to that need. In Carnegie's case, he saw a situation that gave him the notion that raw materials were going to be in demand, and that a new technology was available to help fulfill it.

A few other examples:

- Mark Cuban experienced an **incapability** where he wanted to listen to a radio station not available in his area, and had the **notion** that it might be possible to accomplish this over the internet. This lead to the development of streaming media.
- Sergey Brin and Larry Page saw the **incapability** of hierarchically structured internet search engines to deliver high-quality, relevantly ranked results, and had the **notion** that an algorithmic search engine would be more effective. This lead to the Google search engine.
- Elon Musk saw the **incapability** of current battery technology and had a **notion** of how to improve it significantly so it could be used to power cars and generators. He also saw the problem of costly space launches as an obstacle to commercial space operation, and had a notion of how to make launches much more cost effective.

There are many situations today that allow you to build a notion. Take the Cloud—a situation that has demanded a huge infrastructure build-out as more and more companies migrate to software as a service. Similarly, consider the new driverless technologies, artificial intelligence, and virtual/augmented reality systems—all these will require enormous build-out of storage and processing infrastructure, too. There's plenty more, too. Think of all the incapability and problems that exist in situations like health care, education, training, finance, logistics, transportation, agriculture, communications, space travel, cyber security, energy, care of the aging, and natural resource management.

What major notion might be necessary or possible to improve the world in your area of expertise?

📊 KEY TAKEAWAYS

- This chapter contains four of the most valuable yet difficult skills you can attain: sorting; thinking dynamically; getting effective input from others; and clarifying major notions. Of any section in this book, this is where the quality of your foresight is going to flourish! So make extra effort to drive this home with your team, and put high demands on everyone to burn extra brain energy to get a successful result. Don't walk away with vague, unexciting concepts. Remember Plato's statement, "He who can properly define and divide is to be considered a God." He is speaking to sorting, thinking dynamically, and clarifying.

- The great inventor, Thomas Edison, observed, "There is no expedient to which a man will not resort to avoid the real labor of thinking." I think you will agree this is true, and is a caution you should be aware of.

- "Think!" This was the simple motto of Thomas J. Watson, founder of IBM, and one of the most successful businessmen of all time. I point this out to reinforce what I just said above. To accomplish great results at this stage, you and your team must heed the motto *Think!* I would add, *Think Dynamically!*

💡 TRY THIS

Channel your thinking energy, but don't burn people out. Give them time to re-energize; work in bursts of no distraction for half-hour segments with rests of 10 minutes in between. Have food and snacks and drinks available, because thinking burns a lot of calories. Keep your sessions to a morning if possible, when people are usually more alert. They tend to fade in the afternoon.

Methodically Rate and Rank
the Best Ideas

Obviously, it is useful to have a lot of ideas to choose from, but it can be overwhelming to develop and filter them so that only the gold nuggets remain. A good formula for this is:

Max number of high-quality ideas × max selectivity = Best odds[12]

To narrow it down even further, it is useful to define your wheelhouse to select the best ideas. Naturally you will feel most confident investing in areas you know well, where you can best assess the likelihood of success. In addition, consider your dollar cutoff levels for market size, potential revenue, and initial investment—as these factors will also help you narrow the field.

Ranking Your Concepts

Innovation coach Phil McKinney (philmckinney.com) has developed a simple, effective screening approach for early stage concepts called "The 5 Ranking Questions." They are:

1. Does this idea improve the customer's experience and/or expectations?
    ›   Does it solve a problem?
    ›   Does it offer something needed or wanted?
    ›   Is it novel or unique?

If you want to have good ideas you must have many ideas.

—Linus Pauling, Winner of Nobel Prize in Chemistry, among many awards

There is no passion to be found in playing small - in settling for a life that is less than the one you are capable of living.

—Nelson Mandela

2. Does the idea change how we are positioned competitively in the market?
   > Will it put us ahead of the competition?
   > Will it enhance how the market sees us?
3. Does the idea radically change the economic structure of the industry?
   > Will creation and monetization of value work to our advantage?
4. Do we have a contribution to make?
   > Do we have sufficient experience, expertise and resources to make an impact?
5. Will this idea generate sufficient margins?
   > Are the potential returns attractive given the investment?

You can apply a 1 to 10 scale for each of these 5 criteria, with a grand slam concept scoring 50 points. You will find that criteria #3, radically changing the economic structure of the industry, is difficult to meet for many concepts. I suggest that you want to score criteria #'s 1,2,4, and 5 at least 7 or better to proceed further with a concept. Certainly, you can proceed with lower rated concepts, however I expect you to have difficulty making significant profit with them.

As a test of the effectiveness of this approach, consider a product you know has done well in the market and score it. Then consider another that has not done so well and score it. What difference do you see in results?

A product line I worked closely with scored 45; it did not radically change the economic structure of the industry, but it scored a 10 on the other four criteria, It was hugely profitable for many years. Another product line scored 30; it never took off and the return on investment was modest. The lesson is that you really want to push your team to focus only on highly rated concepts.

As another example, consider the original iPhone. I believe this would have scored a 50, a grand slam. It hit on all cylinders.

Contrast this with the HP TouchPad, a product that was launched in 2011 to compete head-on with the iPad. I believe this product would have scored a 25 at best; it was within HP's capability to make a product for this category, however the TouchPad was not unique, competitive, or market changing. The TouchPad failed quickly and HP discontinued production.

To further reinforce this message, everyone knows of the enormous profitability of the iPhone; it's less well known that HP had to write down over

$800 million of assets and incurred losses of over $700 million because of the TouchPad failure. Pursuing marginal value ideas puts you at peril.

Push for high value opportunities. Don't tie up resources on marginal ideas. If you are short of high value ideas, don't despair. Try to rework them, enhancing user experience, uniqueness, and competitive positioning. Perhaps bring in outside influences to reframe and bring new perspective.

Using the Fermi Method to Ballpark Market Potential

When you have a new business concept, one of the first things you should do is make some back of the envelope calculations about its market potential. The estimate will be rough, but it will give you a feel for whether it is worthwhile pursuing. Enrico Fermi (1901-1954), renowned physicist, gave us a great method of how to solve problems like this; his most famous example is the problem of how to estimate how many piano tuners there are in Chicago. The point of the exercise is to make us realize that we can arrive at a reasonable estimate without having to do a lot of research. Fermi problems typically involve making guesses about quantities and their lower and upper bounds. For instance, just using common sense we could estimate there would be between 20 and 200 tuners without looking at any other data. The steps and some example estimates (not actual facts) are:

1. There are approximately 3,000,000 people living in Chicago.
2. On average, there are two persons in each household in Chicago.
3. Roughly 5% of households have a piano that is tuned regularly.
4. Pianos are tuned on average about once per year.
5. It takes a piano tuner two hours to tune a piano, including travel time.
6. Each piano tuner works eight hours a day, five days a week, fifty weeks a year.

From these assumptions, we roughly estimate that the number of piano tunings per year in Chicago is:

(3,000,000 population of Chicago) ÷ (2 people/household)
× (5% with pianos) × (1 piano tuning per piano per year)
= 75,000 piano tunings per year

The average piano tuner productivity is:

(50 weeks/year) × (5 days/week) × (8 hours/day) ÷ (2 hours to tune a piano) = 1000 piano tunings per year.

Dividing that gives us:

(75,000 piano tunings per year in Chicago) ÷ (1000 piano tunings per year per piano tuner) = 75 piano tuners in Chicago.

The actual number of piano tuners in Chicago is about 130 according to sources at Quora, though some may work part-time. Overall, 75 is a good estimate.

Fermi estimates work because the overestimates and underestimates help to balance each other. If there is no overt bias, a Fermi calculation that involves the multiplication of several estimated factors will likely be more accurate than expected.

Fermi didn't have access to Google; we are usually able to take much of the guesswork out of our estimates today. It's relatively easy to get counts of population sizes, company types and sizes, revenues of industries, number of employees, etc. It is more difficult to estimate how much a target market might buy of a product you want to offer them, though.

In any calculation where you might have a large difference in the upper and lower bound of your guesstimate, Fermi suggested using the geometric mean of the two figures, not the simple arithmetic mean. For instance, if you were to guesstimate that customers would buy between 2 and 20 units each, the arithmetic mean is 11 units (22/2), while the geometric mean is 6.32 (to get that, we multiply the two estimates of 2 and 20 = 40 and take the square root—e.g., $\sqrt{2 \times 20}$). So in this case we would use the 6.32 figure. You can see the practicality of this. Consider a range of 10 to 100, with a simple mean of 55, and a geometric mean of 31.62. The geometric mean helps to keep you from overestimating when you are highly uncertain of the range.

It's important to note again that we are not taking these figures to the bank. We are only trying to determine if we want to take the extra time, effort, and cost to further qualify an opportunity.

A Few Good Men

Once you have roughed out your concept and its market potential, it's time to do a sanity check. The best approach is by discussing it with a few people whom you know to have a good sense of the market you are addressing. They are either key influencers or market mavens. You can find them through internet searches, articles in industry magazines, referrals, and phone calls. Quality of feedback is what you want, not quantity.

They might be salespeople, resellers, end users, consultants—it doesn't really matter what their title is, but they must be insightful and know a lot about what is going on in your area of interest. You can approach them by saying that you have a new idea that could be of benefit to them (having to do with the area of interest to them), and would value their opinion and suggestions. If you feel that you need to protect your concept, ask them to sign a non-disclosure agreement.

This approach can confirm your early notions, or it can save you countless hours working on a concept that is doomed from the get go. As an example of the latter, I once had an idea for a product that might help retailers of perishables to improve management of expiration dates. I located an expert to discuss this, and he explained several reasons why the concept would not fly. Of course, it was disappointing, but I was also relieved that I had not gone through the time and expense of prototyping it.

If I were a young coach today, I would be extremely careful in selecting assistants.

—John Wooden, UCLA basketball coach and winner of 10 national championships

Rough Concept Survey Format

Give your concept a name; it doesn't have to be the final name, but it helps to make it more real.

My approach with an early concept is to discuss it as openly as possible; avoid using just structured questions and checkbox answer formats. This backfires as your interviewees may not understand your idea fully. Try to make it a comfortable conversation, putting the interviewee in the position as the expert you are trying to learn from.

Before meeting or calling the interviewee, provide background information so they can be prepared for a better discussion. For instance, I will send a specification sheet, illustrations, and a benefits summary. If meeting in person, I might have a prototype, a CAD animation or 3D print to show therm.

Start off the conversation with an overview of what you are offering. Place it in the context of key problems you are solving, and the target customer it is designed to help. Discuss your key features in the context of unique benefits you are offering.

Now, listen to them closely. Don't be defensive; you are interested in hearing the truth if this resonates with them. Are they agreeing with you? Are they saying, "Yes, I definitely see where you are going with this," or are they sounding hesitant? Go with their direction, and pursue more clarification of their thoughts. Do not judge their comments or try to put words in their mouths.

Continue the discussion with examples of potential payback/return on investment, or revenue gain, compared to competitive products or alternative approaches. Discuss pricing last. Try to get them to put a value on it. At this early stage, it is important to follow their lead, because it will point you to ideas to improve the concept. Guide them in a general way to a topic and listen. You aren't learning when you're talking.

You will want to listen especially for:

- Their enthusiasm for the concept; how strongly they feel about its potential
- Any concept killer comments; patent issues, legal issues, technical issues, etc.
- Their opinions on competitive advantages/disadvantages of the product
- Suggestions for improvement
- Other problems we didn't address that have high importance to them
- Other people they can refer us to for feedback

Worthwhile Advice from Gordon Gekko

Yes, Gordon Gekko, the despicable character from the movie *Wall Street*, had some good insights mixed in with his bad behavior. Here are the best ones related to refining our best ideas (as written by Stanley Weiser and Oliver Stone):

- I don't throw darts at a board. I bet on sure things.
- Read Sun Tzu, *The Art of War*. Every battle is won before it is ever fought.
- I look at a hundred deals a day. I pick one.
- The most valuable commodity I know of is information.
- I want you to fill in the missing pieces of the puzzle.

With our method, we are following this advice. We are not throwing darts; we look at a lot of ideas, but we are very selective; we get in the flow of valuable information; and we fill in the pieces of the patterns that others don't see.

📊 KEY TAKEAWAYS

- If you have followed the method to this point, you should have at least one very solid, highly-rated concept to pursue. By no means should you accept a lukewarm project as the result of all your work.
- The difference in sales and profit you will achieve with a project rated 40 or more versus 30 or less is exponential. It can be misleading because 10-points difference doesn't seem like a lot. The examples provided make it clear that it is worth striving to reach for the higher level. Strive for 40+.
- Winning the battle before it is fought is foresight at its best.

💡 TRY THIS

Use the five ranking questions rigorously to focus your efforts on concepts that will truly make a difference to your company. Focus and speed of execution are your friends.

5

Adapt the Best Emerging Ideas to Test the Market

ARMED WITH A HIGHLY A RANKED CONCEPT, YOU NEXT WANT TO determine how to adapt and set the stage to your advantage according to market behaviors and power structures. Depending on your area of interest, you will have varying degrees of influence from economic, sociological, technological, and political arenas.

Let's say you work for a company that makes gas pumps or one that operates gas stations. You've discovered that the pace of activity in driverless trucking has quickened. Here is an example of an analysis to adapt an innovation that could be valuable—robotic refueling machines. (The analysis here is purposefully short; it could be expanded to multiple pages if needed). Begin with a table like the one on the next page listing the behavior and power structure qualities.

Next, ask questions such as:

- **What important new traits are emerging?** Driverless (though attended) trucks are already on the road in several states and in parts of Europe. But they are only used for highway driving now. Doing a complete cargo route appears feasible on a restricted geographic basis within two to three years. Once proven this would accelerate quickly.

- **Can you quantify the frequency, magnitude, and timing/ speed?** It is still in the pioneering stages. Proofs of concept are in field operation. It will be a phased-in release with continued attended operation for the next 5 years. Long haul operation will convert first.

If you're not adapting to the very rapidly changing environment, if you can't think creatively, you lose big in this society because there are very few jobs for you left.

—Robert Sternberg, Psychologist and Professor of Human Development, Cornell

Behavioral Influences *Attitudes, beliefs*	Structural Powers *Intensity, centers of influence*
Outlooks, demands, incentives problems, beliefs, attitudes	*Individuals, groups, companies, governments, countries*

	Behavioral Influences	Structural Powers
Economic:	If safety is green-lighted it will result in more vehicles at improving cost of operation reduced insurance costs, and higher demand due to lower collision/ DUI/ fatalities.	In cases where driver is needed for local unloading and inside delivery adoption will be delayed. Of more initial interest to long haulers.
Social:	Robotics are increasingly part of everyday life. If safety is enhanced as seems likely adoption will accelerate.	Trucking executives will be the key influencers in demanding change to fleet operations. We need their input and timelines. Long-haul operators especially.
Technological:	The driverless technology is already viable and will continue to improve.	Robotic refueling would require cooperation with vehicle makers regarding tank/pump interface.
Political:	Unions of truck drivers will resist. Primary concern of government is safety.	There would be new safety regulations regarding automated refueling systems

- **Can you identify the mechanisms that are driving the change?** Improved safety, fewer accidents, much longer hours of operation.
- **What are the implications for future? How will we need to adapt?** The need for robotic re-fuelers will come first from long-haul operators on the interstate highway systems. This looks to be about five years out; however, we need time for development, cooperation with truck makers, regulators, etc.

The goal of the adaptation analysis is to identify stage-setting strategic moves. These could include: collaborations for R&D, joint ventures, acquisitions, licensing, outsourcing, greenfield projects, partnerships/alliances, new channel partners, regulatory support/approval, access to emerging/enabling technology, etc. You must think beyond your current business model and look at what is needed for success, filling in the missing pieces of the puzzle. This will likely mean reaching outside of your company for resources, and getting past the not-invented-here bias that blocks progress.

This type of analysis could also be done from the perspective of truck fleet operators, who would have different concerns especially related to workforce issues, and cost of operations if they were to lag competitors in use of driverless technology.

Predicting Future Market Behaviors with Game Theory

In the model for adaptation above, we looked at the various influences of behaviors and powers that will affect the future of our area of interest. The path forward might be clear, but if it is muddled you will have to use your insight to assess the likely outcomes. For instance, there might be regulatory issues that are yet to be resolved, or economic and political policies that could affect the business.

In a minute, we will sort out the case for driverless trucking more definitively, but first let's look at the best tool for accomplishing this, game theory.

Game theory can be complicated, but there is a useful simplified approach developed by professor-consultant Bruce Bueno De Mesquita (see *The Predictioneer's Game*, 2009). It has been used in hundreds of scenarios with good results. You can use game theory to predict such future changes as health care policy, tax policy, regulatory issues, and negotiation outcomes.

There are four components to the approach.

1. First, we need to establish a baseline of the relevant positions to be considered; in our example, the two extremes are: strongly against driverless trucking, and strongly for driverless trucking. We then rate the positions taken by the relevant players involved on a scale of 0 to 10 as shown in the table below. (In other situations, you might want to rate the positions of players in terms of negotiation outcomes they are seeking or regulatory issues that are being debated).

    Note that these ratings are judgments we make based on our research. Also, keep in mind that the ratings can be dynamic, so if you see a change in positions, influence, etc. you will need to update them.

2. The next component to consider is Influence, by which we rate the varying degrees of influential power of the players involved in the future of our area. In our case, we will consider the influential power of trucking executives, government officials, and driver unions. Influence is rated 0 to 10.

3. Next we want to consider the Priority of the issue to each of the players involved on a 0 to 10 scale, with 10 being the highest possible priority.

4. Lastly we want to rate the Flexibility of the parties to come to an agreement, with wanting an agreement at all costs rated 10, and not willing to budge at all rated 0.

The table below shows a ratings scale summary for the driverless trucking situation.

Position on Issue	Influence	Priority	Flexibility
9-10 Strongly for driverless trucking	9-10 Most persuasive	9-10 Highest priority	9-10 Wants agreement at all cost
7-8 Bias toward driverless	7-8 Highly persuasive	7-8 Important	7-8 Willing to make significant concessions
5-6 Equal mix of driverless and attended driverless	5-6 Persuasive	5-6 One of several priorities	5-6 Fairly flexible
3-4 Bias toward attended driverless	3-4 Moderate influence	3-4 Cares, but not that important	3-4 Willing to make minor concessions
1-2 Only for attended driverless	1-2 Minor influence	1-2 Minor concern	1-2 Strongly values position
0 Strongly against driverless trucking	0 No influence	0 Don't care	0 Won't budge at all

Next we want to put our estimates into a table for calculation. In the table below we have identified the key players and our ratings of their positions, influence, priority, and flexibility. To measure the impact of each player, first multiply the four components as shown in the Column 6. Then add them together for a total sum. Next, because we want to isolate the predicted overall Position, in the Column 7, we multiply the factors excluding Position and add their sums together to arrive at an overall score for Influence, Priority, and Flexibility.

1	2	3	4	5	6	7
Player	Position	Influence	Priority	Flexibility	$P \times I \times P \times F$	$I \times P \times F$
Trucking Execs	9	7	8	9	4,536	504
Government	5	9	7	5	1,575	315
Union	3	6	8	3	432	144
Total					**6,543**	**963**

To isolate the mean Position we are predicting, divide the total of 6,543 by 963 which equals 6.8. Looking at a value of 6.8 (call it 7) on our Position scale means that, using game theory, we can predict a bias toward totally driverless trucking. We expect that the influence of trucking executives and government policy will tilt the balance away from the union position.

Stating the Premises of Your Opportunities

Continuing our analysis of driverless truck implications, we next want to state a premise that we can measure and test. We aren't concerned at this point if it is spot-on accurate. We can modify our premise as we learn more, until we are satisfied that we understand the dynamic that is likely to unfold. Just like Darwin and da Vinci, we can only become more intelligent through error. Let's say that all our work so far has led us make the following premise:

He that would catch fish must venture his bait.

—Benjamin Franklin

> **Premise:** If the safety record of driverless vehicles is proven to reduce accidents and fatalities by at least 60%, then there will be demand for at least 30% of trucks to operate totally unmanned.

We could survey a sample of long haul trucking executives to determine the validity of this premise.

A well-stated premise is a working hypothesis, a prediction of what will happen in certain conditions. If this happens, then that will happen. You are speculating about root cause and effect. A root cause is a reason, not an action. Above, we are speculating from our work that increased safety will be the root cause or reason for driverless trucking to lift off.

Important elements of a premise are: defined variables that are testable, and stated in a way that is falsifiable. In other words, you don't want to state a truism. For example, saying "driverless trucking is going to grow" is a poorly stated working hypothesis because it is already growing. It is not a falsifiable statement and no variables are stated that can be tested.

There should be an independent variable and a dependent variable. The dependent variable (often denoted by y) is one that depends on the value of another; an independent variable (often denoted by x) is one whose variation does not depend on that of another.

Another instance of a poor hypothesis would be, "Sales of driverless trucks are going to be 20% higher at the end of 2017." While this is falsifiable, because sales could be lower than that at the end of the year, a valid independent variable is not stated. The value of sales is the dependent variable we are measuring; but, what are we hypothesizing is going to cause the sales to be higher? The end of the year? Time, alone?

Here's an example of a reasonable premise for a different field altogether, clinical diagnostic software.

> *Premise:* If a computer-based clinical diagnostic system can improve diagnosis accuracy by more than 20%, it will gain acceptance from at least 10% of the medical community.

This premise could be tested with surveys of the medical community.

You can see that word choices are critical when stating your premise. Be as specific as possible.

Here is another example premise: Let's say your observations lead you to determine that there are educational administrators who want to take new approaches to reduce the cost of education while maintaining or improving the quality. You speculate that emerging technology in artificial intelligence and virtual/augmented reality is going to allow the classroom to be extended in ways that will reduce the physical cost of professors and buildings. You also are aware that change in education comes slowly. This is an expensive undertaking and you need confirmation that there will be sufficient demand before starting development.

A possible premise from your discovery findings would be:

> *Premise:* If university administrators had access to a system that could deliver a virtual interactive classroom experience for 30% of their courses (questions from students would be answered through highly prepared artificial intelligence software, with input from leading professors in the country), at an annual savings of $50,000 per course offered, then at least 20% of university administrators would be willing to purchase it.

This premise could be tested with personal surveys, phone surveys, surveys at administrator events, etc.

Another example I can offer is a situation where a computer printer manufacturer I worked at was considering the design of a new feature set that would require considerable time and expense. We observed situations in the field that had given us the idea in the first place, but wanted to be sure there would be sufficient demand before proceeding. From surveys, we determined that a significant number of users would indeed benefit from the new design. The resulting product was highly successful. As a side benefit, the survey information was also very helpful in the creation of sales messages and marketing materials.

Some other points to consider here are that if your surveys do not support your premise, you could at least learn something that leads you to a new premise. Also, it could be that the timing of your idea is wrong, and that you could revisit it when conditions are different in a year or two.

I have tested many ideas that didn't show enough demand to make investment worthwhile. But, think of the time and money saved that was directed to better ideas instead!

📊 KEY TAKEAWAYS

- If your concepts are truly innovative, there likely are missing pieces of the puzzle that you will need to fill in. The adaptation analysis will clarify those.
- You likely will need to reach outside of your company to find the pieces of the puzzle.
- Defining the premise of your concept is critical. This will be easier if you have done a thorough job: sorting; thinking dynamically; getting effective input from others; and clarifying major notions.

6

Calculate the Risks and Rewards Before Going All In

T HE HIGHER THE UNCERTAINTY THE HIGHER THE RISK. BUT WHERE does uncertainty come from? From two areas.

If you think too long on your next step, you will end up in life standing on one leg.

—Chinese Proverb

1. Lack of knowledge about a terrain (we say, "I don't know this area.")

    Risk = Low knowledge

2. Inability to determine the possible consequences and likelihoods of a course of action.

    High risk = Low knowledge × Unknown potential impact

At this point you will have significant market knowledge, thereby reducing risk of your venture significantly. Still, you need to measure the potential financial payback and return on investment.

Numerous studies have shown that we overestimate our ability to predict. Studies also show that people do irrational things, make irrational choices, and often act differently than they say they will. So our measurements, particularly of behavior, aren't ever perfect or certain. In fact, Heisenberg's Uncertainty Principle says that the act of measuring, in and of itself, affects results in unknown ways.

Still, we need to measure if we don't want to be in a state of total uncertainty. Probabilities help us to accomplish this by putting our measurements into ranges of likelihood. My goal here is to point you to some simple techniques you can use to reduce uncertainty. There are more sophisticated techniques that can be used when necessary, but for our purposes, we are mostly interested in accomplishing a few things:

- We want to validate the premises we have for market acceptance of our concept.
- We want to determine if demand for our new product or service will exceed our minimum levels to warrant further investment.
- We want to determine the risk of losing our money as well as our upside for gain.

The key pieces of information we need are:

1. The total potential number of customers in the niche markets we plan to address
2. The percentage of those customers who are likely to buy our offering
3. The amount ($'s, units) of our offering those customers will buy, and
4. The amount of upfront investment we expect to spend developing and launching our offering

When We Already Have Adequate Data

How we approach the screening of our premise depends on the amount of prior knowledge we have. If we are exploring a market that is already defined by competitors and users, and data sources are available for our estimates, the job is easier than if we are considering an emerging new area. For instance, to expand into a new geography with our current products, it will be relatively easy to estimate potential sales based on our knowledge of the market in our own geography.

Making an estimate of the potential demand for a totally new offering is quite different, though; you will have to conduct market surveys unless you can find a source that has already done the work. This is possible and worth considering, though you likely will have to pay for the information, which can be quite expensive ($2,500 to $5,000) for a report that is also being sold to other interested parties. If you want an edge, I suggest conducting your own surveys even if you buy a third-party report, because it will give you a unique perspective unavailable to potential competitors.

If you already have considerable insight about potential market demand, you could use Bayes theorem, which allows you to make probability estimates based on your knowledge and intuition to determine the likelihood of a result.

For instance, you can estimate the likelihood that a minimum % of customers will buy, given that you have a certain % confidence level that the market is dissatisfied with current offerings.

Note that what we are doing here is using cause and effect analysis; instead of just saying that you are X% confident that you will meet the minimum requirement, you are saying that your ability to do this is conditional. It is dependent on another factor, so you need to take this into account as well. Also, keep in mind that you are never 100% confident. This process forces you to make our decision criteria more explicit, and to uncover any weaknesses in your understanding of the market.

The formula for Bayes calculation is: $P(A|B) = P(A) \times P(B|A)/P(B)$

To make Bayes calculations for our purpose of determining if more than a certain % will buy, we need three input probabilities defined below:

1. Probability A or P(A) = The probability that at least X% will buy (X being our minimum cutoff)
2. Probability B or P(B) = The probability that at least a certain % of the market is not satisfied with current offerings
3. Probability of B given A or P(B|A) = The conditional probability of the market not being satisfied with current offerings given that at least X% will buy

The value we want to solve for is the probability of A given B or P (A|B). In other words, we want to know the probability that at least a certain % will buy, given that at least a certain % of the market is not satisfied with current offerings.

In our case, we will want to make at least two Bayes calculations; one to determine if we are likely to exceed our minimum market penetration objective, and the other to determine if the average purchase quantity per customer is likely to exceed our minimum objective.

So let's say that we have done considerable research and have come to the following conclusions about probabilities of market demand for a concept:

P(A) = Probability that at least 10% of the market will buy = 50%
P(B) = Probability that over half of the market is not satisfied with current offerings = 50%
P(B|A) = Probability of B given A is true = 60%
P(A|B) = Probability A given B = 50% × (60%/50%) = 60%

We are then 60% confident that we can meet our minimum market penetration objective. This is a solid go ahead if other factors line up as well. Considering that only about 30% of venture-backed startups survive in some form, this level of confidence would be exceptional. (The risk-reward payoff will be discussed later.)

Let's look next at the minimum average unit sales required. Say we have determined that 10 units average per customer is our minimum threshold, and we have data from our research that gives us insight about the reasonableness of this figure:

$P(A)$ = Probability to sell 10 units average = 50%
$P(B)$ = Probability that at least 10% of the market will buy = 60% (from above calculation)
$P(B|A)$ = Probability of B given A is true = 70%
$P(A|B)$ = Probability A given B = 50% × (70%/60%) = 58.3%

At this point we are 58% confident that we can meet our minimum sales objectives. Whether we want to proceed will depend on the ROI payback we expect; we will show how to evaluate this in the upcoming section *Calculating ROI of Projects* section. (At a 60% confidence level you will want to expect at least a 3 to 1 return on investment).

What to Do When You Don't Have Adequate Data

Despair ruins some, presumption many.

—Benjamin Franklin

If you do not have the prior knowledge or information to do the Bayes calculations, you can conduct buyer surveys to get it. You might be surprised that it is possible to improve your forecast confidence substantially with relatively small sample sizes of 30 or fewer people.

Before organizing a buyer survey, I highly recommended writing a draft sales letter to the target buyer. Write the letter as if you were depending on it to spark their interest in your offering. Discuss all the relevant features, and more importantly the benefits they will receive when they buy the product or service. Disclose the price, and justify it. Offer a guarantee. Talk about your credibility. By going through this process, you will be forced to think about all of the questions an intelligent buyer is going to have in order to give you answers. When you are satisfied with your letter show it to some associates for feedback, and tweak it as necessary.

Next you should test it on a few of your target buyers either on the phone or in-person if possible. You can set it up by explaining to them that you are planning to introduce a product/service that could be of benefit to them, and that you would greatly appreciate their feedback on it. Don't read the letter to them; give them an overview of your offering, its benefits, and the problems it is intended to solve. Listen closely to their questions and comments to determine if they bring to light something you might have missed. If you can provide them with some visual aids (diagrams, illustrations, prototypes) so much the better.

By this point you should have a good feel for how to present your offering effectively, and a good grasp of the most important questions you need to ask your market. Now you can target a mix of buyers (some large, some small) with your survey on a larger scale. I have always used a mix of phone and personal interviews, sometimes offering a gift with a value of $100 or less for an in-person meeting (tickets to events, gift cards, a donation to a charitable cause of their choice, etc.). Do not make it a sales call even though you are going to ask them for a soft commitment to a purchase intent. If they are truly excited by what you are offering, it will be obvious; they will start asking you questions about how fast they can get it!

For my screening work, I do not need 95% or higher confidence. I might decide later that I want to do larger scale studies with higher confidence, but for now a 90% confidence level is sufficient. When I say 90% confident, it means I recognize that my sample data has a margin of error, but I have tried to account for that by saying my average results fall into a range of possibilities. For instance, based on a sample survey, I might find that customers want to buy an average of 6 units; however, depending on our sample size, and the variability of the units demanded (i.e., some want 2, some want 12), I might say with 90% confidence that the true average is between 3 and 9.

There are mathematical calculations you can make to determine the ranges of confidence; but for those of us who are not "mathletes," there are tools you can use with no calculation necessary. These were developed by statistician Douglas Hubbard, and are discussed in his book, *How To Measure Anything*.[13] The tools are designed especially for relatively small sample sizes of 30 or fewer respondents.

The first small sample risk reduction technique is called the Mathless 90% Confidence Interval. This can be most useful for measuring the amount ($'s, units) that customers will buy. Using the table below, all you need to do is match the sample size with the number you should use to select the nth smallest and nth largest values from your sample survey to determine your 90% confidence range of the median value.

Sample Size	nth smallest and largest sample value to use
5	1st
8	2nd
11	3rd
13	4th
16	5th
18	6th
21	7th
23	8th
26	9th
28	10th
30	11th

Here is an example. Say you have taken a sample of 8 people asking how many units they will buy; the answers are 3, 5, 5, 6, 8, 9,10, 11. Go down the left-hand column for sample size 8, and look across to see that you will take the 2nd smallest and 2nd largest sample value, which are 5 and 10. You can be 90% confident that the median purchase will be between 5 and 10 units. Or say that you ask the same question of 16 people; the answers are 3, 4, 4, 5, 6, 6, 6, 7, 8, 8, 9, 10,10, 11, 12,12. Using the table for 16 sample size, you see that you take the 5th smallest and 5th largest responses. You can be 90% confident that the median purchase size will be between 6 and 10 units.

In the above example, if you need a median demand of at least 4 units you would be pleased to see it is higher than that. If you need it to be 15 units you would see it is considerably short. Once you get past 30 samples the incremental change of added data to the median value will be small. Please note the Mathless 90% interval provides the median value, which is the midpoint where half of the responses are above and half are below. This can be different than the average (or mean value). In the series 5, 6, 7, 8, 9, 10, 20 for example, the median is 8, and the mean is 9.29

Another easy-to-use technique is the Population Proportion 90% for Small Samples. This is useful for measuring absolute sample counts (rather than sample values as the Mathless 90% does), and can determine if you are confident of meeting your minimum market penetration objectives. Let's say you have an objective that at least 10% of your market needs to be interested in your offering. You sample 20 potential customers and find that 6 of them are interested (30% of your small sample is interested). Is this proof enough?

Using the Small Samples lower boundary chart below, we find that for a sample size of 20 with 6 responses that we are 90% confident that the lower bound proportion is 18%. So your offering does exceed the 10% minimum level of interest you require. If we had a sample size of 30, and 14 were interested in buying, we would be 90% confident that at least 33% are interested.

Population Proportion 90% Confidence Intervals - Lower Boundary

# Responses	2	4	6	8	10	12	14	16
Sample Size								
10	8%	20%	30%					
20	5%	10%	18%	25%	33%			
30	3%	7%	10%	15%	22%	27%	33%	37%

Calculating the ROI of Projects

No matter how diligent you are, there is going to be risk that your concept could fail. It might be due to execution, unforeseen competition, product performance problems, or other issues. To offset the risk of new product launches and new ventures, it is necessary to earn a rate of return on investment (ROI) commensurate with that risk. There is not a particular ROI figure that is considered standard; it is a corporate decision as to what is acceptable. I give you some rough rules of thumb later in this section.

A helpful tool for looking at the risk of your investment is the Kelly Calculator. Warren Buffett and other investing legends have found this to be a useful tool. It uses your assessments of paybacks and probabilities to determine how much investment to put at risk, and calculates an average rate of return. Rather than go into its detailed workings, I suggest you simply visit a web site http://www.albionresearch.com/kelly/default.php that has a Kelly calculator.

Efficiency innovations provide return on investment in 12-18 months. Empowering innovations take 5-10 years to yield a return.

—Clayton Christensen

The calculator asks you to enter three key figures:

- your bankroll for investment;
- your estimated odds for payback (is it 10 to 1 where you get back $10 for every $1 invested, or 5 to 1?); and,
- your estimated probability of winning as a percentage (is it 30% or 60%? Your surveys should help to guide you.)

For example, with a $1 mil investment bankroll; a potential 5 to 1 payback; and a 40% chance of a successful result, the Kelly calculator recommends at most a $280,000 investment. It also reports:

- On 40% of similar occasions, you would expect to gain $1,400,000 in addition to your stake of $280,000 being returned.
- But on those occasions when you lose, you will lose your stake of $280,000.
- Your fortune will grow, on average, by about 15.31% on each bet.

But, look what happens when you increase the probability of success to 60%:

- According to the Kelly criterion your optimal bet is about 52% of your capital, or $520,000.
- On 60% of similar occasions, you would expect to gain $2,600,000 in addition to your stake of $520,000 being returned.
- But on those occasions when you lose, you will lose your stake of $520,000.
- Your fortune will grow, on average, by about 47.5% on each bet.

The average rate of return jumps from 15.3% to 47.5%. This is a huge difference in results based on 20% higher certainty! This goes to show that information, harnessed effectively, has enormous value.

In the table below, I show the calculated return on investment for a series of payback ratios at different levels of probability of success. In general, it illustrates that you must anticipate very high payback ratios when your probability of success is below 50%. Think about this when you invest in the stock market, too. When you pick a stock, what do you expect it to return to you, and how confident in success are you? The Kelly calculator says that even if you are 60%

confident that you will double your money (get a 1:1 payback), your average rate of return on a series of such investments will only be 2%. Now this may be conservative, because it assumes when you lose, that you lose your entire stake which may not be true for stocks because you can sell them when the price declines too far. But the Kelly calculator is generally insightful and useful.

This goes to show why Peter Lynch, one of the most successful stock pickers of all time when he ran the Fidelity Magellan fund, said that he looked for "10-baggers." He was looking for 10:1 payback stock opportunities. Lynch was also known to spend a lot of time in the field, not behind a desk. He used to call in some of his buy and sell orders from pay phones. He would scout out new businesses, take the pulse of salespeople and resellers, visit stores, talk to customers and competitors, etc.—anything to give him an edge in foresight.

% Probability	30%	40%	50%	60%
Payback:				
1:1	No go	No go	No go	2%
2:1	No go	1%	6%	15%
3:1	1%	5%	15%	27%
4:1	3%	10%	22%	38%
5:1	5%	15%	29%	48%
10:1	18%	34%	55%	80%
20:1	34%	57%	85%	117%

The table also shows why venture capitalists insist on driving exponential results from their investments. When you consider that only about 30% of their investments survive in some form, they really need to be looking for 20:1 paybacks or higher. Even a 10-bagger isn't enough to get them excited.

If you are looking for a more straightforward approach to estimate your payback, you can simply look at expected values of payback using this formula:

(Probability of Gain × $ Expected Amount of Gain) − (Probability of Loss × Expected Amount of Loss).

For a stock investment example let's say you invest $10,000. You expect the stock to double for a $10,000 gain with 50% confidence. You set a stop loss at $5,000, so you will not risk losing your entire stake. Your expected value is:

50% × \$10,000 expected gain = \$5,000 net expected gain
Less 50% × \$5,000 expected loss = \$2,500 net expected loss
= a net expected gain of \$2,500

If you could make a number of such investments over time, earning \$2,500 on \$10,000, you would be quite happy, making an average return of 25%. In the real world, however, consistently having 50% success with stocks doubling before giving back 50% is not common.

While the ability to stop losses affects results positively, with a new product concept or startup this is not a good assumption to make. If things go south, it is best to assume that losses will be total. The Kelly calculator assumes total loss, so it is a helpful guide to new product investing.

Taking a Deeper Dive if Necessary

Everything yields to diligence.

—Antiphanes

Once you are at a point of commitment to move forward with a course of action, it is useful to do a deep dive like what Richard Branson did when he entered the airline industry with Virgin Airlines. Branson said that he spent roughly 3 months with his team learning every single aspect of the business from flight operations, to ticketing and reservations, scheduling, meals, entertainment, seating, equipment, baggage handling, etc. If you are entering a new area and/or one that is going to require substantial investment, you will likely want to do a deep dive and immerse yourself with other team members into the environment.

As a metaphor for why this should be done, think about Jack London's 1903 book, *Call of the Wild*, in which a small group of people went to Alaska during the Gold Rush. They had worked out their plans on paper without ever having gone to the area to get a firsthand view of the terrain. They knew nothing about working with sled dogs, survival in the cold wilderness, etc. They were determined to find gold and had a plan. When they arrived in Alaska they were warned numerous times from the start that they were going about it all wrong. All of their planning assumptions were wrong, and they ignored warnings about the safety of the trail and ice pack. No surprise, the group perished.

The lesson is to not let our enthusiasm for a new venture cloud our view of reality that expertise is required to succeed. To become an expert, you need to dive in deeply to understand the baggage handling, the ticketing, how to work with sled dogs, and when you are on thin ice. Make a final reality check by determining all the things you must avoid because they would make your project fail. For example, you must NOT:

1. Be generic
2. Over discount
3. Underestimate competitors or new competitors you might encounter
4. Overpromise to customers and employees
5. Hire employees with a poor fit
6. Underestimate costs and overestimate revenue
7. Run out of cash

You will likely have other "avoid at all costs" issues. Clearly, you want to focus on what you need to do to make the project a success, but listing out these issues to avoid can make you stop to consider if you have missed any critical items.

📊 KEY TAKEAWAYS

- The work you are doing with the foresight method is rarely done well by others, if at all. I imagine that is why the rate of product and business failure is high. You are increasing your odds of success greatly. And gaining competitive advantage.
- Risk cannot be eliminated entirely; however, you can offset risk with high reward over time if you pick your projects well.
- Make the extra effort to take a deeper dive when you have zeroed in on a new concept or venture. Do a reality check, and make a list of the things you absolutely must not let happen because they would sink the project.

7

Make a Successful Market Entry

WITH A SOLID BUSINESS CONCEPT IN HAND, YOUR SUCCESS in launching it will depend primarily on a handful of points of execution. This presumes that you are offering a high-quality product at an acceptable price, and that you have sufficient funding. These are the execution issues to be concerned about:

There are no secrets to success. It is the result of preparation, hard work, and learning from failure.

—Colin Powell

Team: A well-rounded team with complementary talents in marketing, sales, finance, and operations is ideal. There should be talents in creativity, business systems and processes, analysis and strategy, and working with people inside and outside the company.

Focus of resources: Eliminating wasted effort is important for a startup operation. A disciplined approach of time and money management is critical. I have seen startups burn through cash quickly by spending on unnecessary items. You should set funds aside for unexpected events, opportunities, or problems.

High value targeting: You need an understanding of the concentration of business in your markets, the key buying influencers, and the best way to focus on high quality prospects. This will make an enormous difference to your results.

Making a strong offer: A strong offer states a benefit and a payoff that you know is of high interest to your customer, and gives them options to engage with you in a non-threatening conversation. People have their guard up when they sense a strong sales pitch coming, or when asked to provide a lot of information before even having a discussion. They are also often reluctant to sign up for email lists because they get so much junk mail.

Therefore, it is important for you to ask only pertinent qualifying questions, and to give options for people to communicate with you. For instance, initially you don't need to know everything about them. You really want to know if they have the problem you are trying to address and how urgent it is for them to address it. Once you initiate a conversation, you can ask them for more detailed information so that you can determine how best to help them.

Ensuring satisfaction: It can be all-encompassing getting new customers, so much so that we lose sight of our current ones. To stay in business for the long run, you need repeat purchases from your customer base. You want to foster loyalty and word of mouth referrals, as they are by far the most effective advertising for you. Make the extra effort to follow up on customer purchases to ensure that you are meeting or exceeding expectations. If anything is amiss, act quickly to correct it. I have seen companies go out of business because they failed to correct a serious quality problem soon enough.

The Market Pyramid

For many products and services, a relatively small number of customers accounts for a disproportionately high percentage of sales. This typically holds true for the market and for your customer base. You should allocate your resources and activities accordingly. For example, let's say you are targeting a niche with 5,000 customers that you believe has a total potential for sales of $100 million (over time).

From your research, you determine that 250 (5%) of those customers will account for $30 million (30%), for an average of $120,000 each. As you work your way down through the pyramid, you find that 3,250 (65%) of the customers will account for $20 mil, for an average of $6,153 each. Clearly, you must manage your media and sales resource mix to address these vastly different potential opportunities. You must make it your priority to be known to the top of the pyramid!

The Market Influencers Chart

When you have identified and prioritized the top of the pyramid, you also must recognize that the purchase of our product or service will likely be influenced by multiple job functions within your prospective client's company. It helps to make a visual of their functions, interests, and influence like the one below. The idea is that different functions will need to hear different messages from you. The CEO needs to be convinced that you are going to improve return on investment, increase sales, and so on, while the CIO wants to know how you are going to improve uptime, ease of use and, service. Be sure to think about all the functions you need to get onboard with you.

We're looking for influencers within every marketplace, who are the people who help influence decision-makers within that community.

—Keith Belling, founder of popchips

Decision Factor	CEO	CFO	CIO	CMO	etc.
Power	10	5	7	9	
Reliability			★		
ROI	★				
Cost		★			
Performance				★	
Ease of use			★	★	
Speed of service			★		
Increase in revenue	★			★	
Decrease in costs	★	★			
Higher productivity	★				
etc					

Four Power Steps to Segmenting Your Market

I wish I had a dollar for every time I've come across a company that opts out when it comes to obtaining high quality list sources for marketing and sales. Expensive sales people are hired and told, "Go get 'em tiger. Go out and make it rain!" Wrong idea. It doesn't work that way.

A problem I often see here is that many functions in a company, including top management, are begrudging of salespeople. They think that salespeople live off the work of everyone else, yet they get the accolades, awards, commissions, etc. They think, "Why should we give them great sales leads? Shouldn't they have to dig up their own leads? Why make it easy for them?"

The Internet is really about highly specialized information, highly specialized targeting.

—Eric Schmidt, chairman of Alphabet, Google's parent company

Watch the movie *Glengarry Glen Ross* (based on the Pulitzer prize and Tony Award winning play by David Mamet) for a dramatic demonstration of how good sales leads make a difference in life. Poor sales results hurt everyone in the company. If there is begrudging about the salespeople, it is a sign of dysfunctional management. Sales is a team effort, and there needs to be investment in high-quality information to keep the salespeople from spinning their wheels chasing after poorly qualified prospects.

Power segmenting can make the difference in getting up to a 20% hit rate on your prospecting versus the 1% or less that is typical. Your sales and marketing effectiveness will increase tremendously when you take four steps to segment your potential customers.

1. Business Demographics. This first level of segmentation uses widely available data such as industry type, number of employees, location, and estimated revenue. Sales prospecting value is minimal. An enterprise software company, for example, would find a list of manufacturers in the Midwest with 1,000 to 5,000 employees somewhat helpful, but still largely unqualified.

2. Company Characteristics. This next level segmentation considers factors that indicate a higher propensity to buy. Depending on the product or service you are selling, this might include: total number of locations; number of salespeople; number of desk workers; sales growth rate; and functions on-site (i.e., accounting, production). An example would be to target manufacturing companies in the Midwest with 1,000 to 5,000 employees that have a certain amount of warehousing square footage. Now we're helping the sales reps to zero in on better prospects.

3. Special Conditions. This is highly valuable for segmenting and can include factors such as: types and quantities of equipment installed; level of technological sophistication; key software and applications used, etc. Continuing with the Midwest manufacturing example, you might want to screen for prospects that do not yet have manufacturing enterprise software installed.

4. Decision-Maker Profile. The ultimate level of segmentation adds this criteria to the mix. In this case, you target executives and managers with known purchase involvement in your product area. Other criteria might include: annual spending in your category; brand preferences; and recent purchases. At this level of segmentation, a sales rep might, for instance, focus on prospects that meet the previous criteria and have IT budgets of $1 million or more.

Think of the extra revenue you could generate with this approach compared to the low probability prospecting most companies do. The productivity of a salesperson can get a big boost just from pointing them at the right targets. For instance, a large commercial finance company rated prospects on six criteria and found that the highest rated 30% of those were three times more likely to do business with them than the remaining 70%. Their overall conversion/ close rate increased 20% as a result.

The most extreme example of the power of this approach I have personally encountered is with a company that does project management services. This firm has over $160 mil in sales through only six salespeople/project managers. These people are paid a straight commission of 5% of revenue, so they make an average of $1.3 mil each annually. Their customers are almost exclusively the largest companies in the world. Far from begrudging their incomes, the president of this company invests heavily in making them better with ongoing coaching and training.

Making a Strong Offer and Keeping the Engagement Going

Each of us has a gift, a talent, that we can offer to the world that makes the world essentially a better place.

—James Redfield, author

In addition to having a well-identified target customer, the next most important thing you can do is make a strong offer for the customer to engage in a dialogue with you. You want the customer to hear your entire story. To accomplish this, you must have a good sense for the level of attention that is reasonable to expect from the customer's point of view. Here are two recommendations:

First, keep in mind when communicating with potential customers is that you are not creating demand. You are fulfilling a demand that is already there. Your message must relate in a way that shows you understand the potential customer's desires, needs, and goals. He or she must feel and believe that you identify with them. Also, they must believe that you will respect their space and not bombard them with constant calls, emails, etc. that have no value.

Second, know that your potential customers are in various stages of awareness and interest in your product category. The awareness runs from:

- Highly aware, intends to buy soon
- Generally aware of various solutions, still fuzzy about buying
- Aware of and frustrated with the problem, but not aware of solutions
- Unaware that there is a real problem with possible solutions

You must tailor your approach to these groups because they have different information needs. For instance, while the most urgent buyers will respond well to highly directed offers of price and persuasion, the others will not. People who are fuzzy about buying might best be budged off the fence with a promise or money back guarantee. People at even lower levels of awareness and interest likely need stories, shocking facts, and expert opinions to get them engaged.

Once you get potential customers engaged, realize that only about 15% of them are going to buy (from someone) within 90 to 120 days. This is typical; your results may vary so you should track this. The remaining 85% will buy (from someone) within 18 months. It is critical that you have a process, automated ideally, to maintain appropriate contact with this group. Always let the prospects know the next action steps to take. And track your buckets, or cohorts, as they go through the sales funnel to measure your effectiveness at conversion.

The biggest obstacle you face is inertia for the customer to do nothing. With a strong benefit and payoff headline, you will appeal to people who have urgent awareness of the problem and desire to solve it. With others, you will have to educate them about your offering. In doing so you must establish credibility, belief, and trust. News stories, case histories, seminars, white papers, webinars, and testimonials can be effective image builders.

Along with your offer, you should also make a promise of satisfaction to reduce the customer's risk of disappointment in the purchase. It also can be helpful to give the prospect something to interact with such as a sample, a demonstration, or a form that they can fill in the blanks with their data to calculate a payback or return on investment. I have used these with great results.

Customers can be a good sounding board for your marketing communications messages. They can tell you if your messaging is attention-getting and relevant enough before you commit to it. They bring a perspective that can be difficult for you to relate to. Being the senders, it can be hard to put ourselves in the position of the receiver.

Make it a priority to test, test, test different offers and list sources. Track the results and measure the cost of a lead versus its sales results. A lead that appears to be expensive to generate can be well-worth the cost, especially if you expect a long-term customer relationship.

Cost of Customer Acquisition

The cost of customer acquisition (CAC) is critical, and is a reason for failure in many businesses. It is as important as product cost, but often it is not as well understood and therefore isn't calculated.

An out of balance business model

Source: David Skok, for Entrepreneurs website, www.forentrepreneurs.com

The calculation of your CAC simply involves adding up all of your sales and marketing costs that are directed at new customer acquisition (not for maintenance of existing customers), and dividing that by the number of new customers actually gained. Then you must compare that figure to the average lifetime profit value (LTV) you expect from a customer. Clearly you need for the LTV to be greater than the CAC for the business to stay viable, otherwise you will burn through cash endlessly.

For a startup, the ratio will be low at first. It might be a 1 to 1 ratio of marketing cost to new sales, but once you are in business for several years, the cost as a percentage of sales should drop significantly. You should look for a LTV to CAC ratio of at least 3 to 1, and ideally 5 to 1. Also, ideally look for recovery of costs within the first year of sales to the customer. At a 5 to 1 ratio your CAC is running at 20% of new sales. These figures vary widely depending on your business. It some cases CAC can be $10, in others $100,000. The key is the balance with LTV.

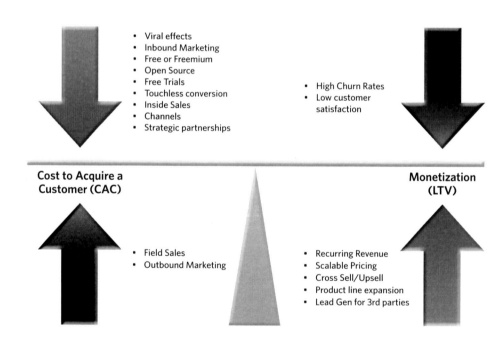

- Viral effects
- Inbound Marketing
- Free or Freemium
- Open Source
- Free Trials
- Touchless conversion
- Inside Sales
- Channels
- Strategic partnerships

- High Churn Rates
- Low customer satisfaction

Cost to Acquire a Customer (CAC)

Monetization (LTV)

- Field Sales
- Outbound Marketing

- Recurring Revenue
- Scalable Pricing
- Cross Sell/Upsell
- Product line expansion
- Lead Gen for 3rd parties

Source: David Skok, for Entrepreneurs website, www.forentrepreneurs.com

The Cause of Wasted Marketing $'s

Vague definitions of target markets and customers are the main cause of wasted resources.

To sell to our market efficiently, there must be readily identifiable and reachable customers, otherwise we have an inefficient, wasteful shotgun approach. This seems logical, but it is violated all the time. For example, let's say that you identify your customers as being interested in "high quality." The difficulty with this is that it is vague, and not of much help in directing focused efforts of sales and marketing resources.

When profiling your target customers gather as much measurable data as you can about them that can be used to zero in on the best prospects, then search out list and media sources that can help you to pinpoint them more precisely. This can make the difference in getting high response to your efforts instead of subpar (i.e., less than 1%, meaning you wasted 99% of your spend).

No problem can be solved until it is reduced to some simple form. The changing of a vague difficulty into a specific, concrete form is a very essential element in thinking.

—J. P. Morgan

Important Rules of Channel Management

If you have difficulty entering new markets or growth has stalled in your existing markets, you might have violated important rules of channel management. Reasons you are struggling could include: poor channel partner selection criteria, unrealistic expectations, low commitment of resources, or limited exchange of information. The following guidelines will help you to identify potential problems with your channel program.

Channel partners are implementers of marketing strategy, not creators of it. Many manufacturers mistakenly expect their channel partners to create and implement marketing strategies for their assigned territories. The problem is that channel partners are typically organized around providing sales, service, and order fulfillment functions, not marketing. Channel partners are accustomed to filling demand that has been created by the marketing programs of the manufacturers they represent.

It is a bad practice to let channel partners control the marketing strategy for your company. You should lead your own marketing strategy development and make local adjustments with the input of the channel partners. In order to lead, you need a good understanding of the needs and buying behaviors of end-users. Get this understanding through desk and field research of the market. This requires extra time and cost, but the alternatives of guessing about user needs or turning over control to channel partners are not acceptable; they are the easy way out and will result in poor performance.

Manufacturers should select channel partners, not the other way around. Too often manufacturers are attracted to channel partners who approach them with immediate sales opportunities. While it is difficult to turn away sales opportunities, the selection of a channel partner should be a strategic decision based on a market assessment, not a reaction to a channel partner inquiry.

Hastily formed relationships usually falter in the long run. Typically a channel partner who hints at an immediate sales opportunity already carries competing lines of products. In these cases, the channel partner will be in the driver's seat, playing the competing manufacturers off of each other, likely keeping growth of your product line in check. For this reason, the "obvious" channel partner choice isn't always the best choice. The strongest relationships in the long run are formed with channel partners who carry complementary, rather than competing product lines.

It is important that your channel partner fit well with your company values and strategies. This is more important than immediate fit with the market. You will probably be more successful in the long run by working with a channel partner that doesn't have immediate opportunities, but does have high interest in your company; is compatible with your values; is willing to invest in training and market development; and has complementary rather than competing lines of products. It is a warning sign if a potential channel partner is reluctant to invest in sales and technical training for your products. Another warning sign is when the poorly trained channel partner complains that you need to cut prices to win sales.

Shared commitment of resources is a key to successful market entry. It takes money, people and persistence to get through the uncertain startup phases of a new market. The channel partner cannot be expected to shoulder the entire burden of startup costs. If you place all financial responsibility on the channel partner, they will not be as cooperative with you as they would be otherwise.

Have a candid discussion with the channel partner about the resources that will be committed by each party to develop the market. Advertising, promotion, and publicity are required to create awareness. Extensive training is needed to perform sales and service professionally. It may be necessary to invest in a service infrastructure before sales are significant. Don't wait until after signing an agreement with a channel partner to deal with these issues. If the channel partner will not make shared commitments you should continue searching for a better partner.

Continual flow of information is needed to make sound decisions. Many channel programs fail over time because channel partners are unwilling to provide information to manufacturers about their activities. From the start, you should make clear to your channel partners that you require certain information from them on a regular basis to make effective decisions about your *mutual* business interests. This includes sales reports with customer and pricing information, number of leads generated from marketing activities, quotes/proposals prepared, etc. Don't make the reporting requirements overwhelming; limit them to the best indicators you know of that are predictors of future business activity.

Encourage the exchange of ideas to stimulate creative solutions. It is helpful for channel partners to see how their counterparts are succeeding. Encourage channel partners to share their experiences with new customer applications, successful advertising and promotional campaigns, effective new sales tactics, and complementary product and service offerings. Success stories are motivating to channel partners and give them fresh ideas to increase sales.

Trust and commitment of both parties make a manufacturer/channel partner partnership successful. With trust and commitment, the sharing of values, resources, and information naturally follow. I have consistently seen small channel partners who were true partners far outsell large channel partners who were not loyal partners, often by a factor of 10 times or more.

Creating Customer Stickiness

Once you attain a relationship with a customer, you need to keep them. To do this, it is critical that you maintain trust and reliability. Customers need to trust that you will keep your commitment to their satisfaction, and know that they can depend on you to deliver as promised. These are the fundamentals, and without them no business will prosper.

Creating "stickiness" is a way of defining actions you can take to build intense customer loyalty. In general, you can expect more loyalty when your customer requires a high level of quality, and product and service integration into their operations. Loyalty is much harder to foster when assortment, wide availability, and low price are most important.

There is only one boss. The customer. And he can fire everybody in the company from the chairman on down, simply by spending his money somewhere else.

—Sam Walton

These are some of the sticky offerings you should consider, especially for your largest customers:

1. Eliminating risk of purchase upfront - this is an easy way to establish trust
2. Switching costs - work to your favor when you are the incumbent; when trying to replace an incumbent it can help for you to defray the customer's cost of switching to you
3. Service options - the more the better; onsite, mail-in, walk-in, emergency on call, etc.
4. Guarantees - extended warranties, lifetime, etc.
5. Training - help users to get the best performance from your products
6. Documentation - can head off a lot of problems for users and service repair techs; will reduce support calls and increase customer satisfaction
7. Financing - leasing, 0% interest, terms
8. Design options - allow users to customize by bundling or unbundling optional features
9. Inventory management, offsite storage, just in-time delivery; often desirable for components, supplies and packaging materials
10. Customization - example would be software tweaks for compatibility with legacy systems
11. Tech support access - around the clock, web, phone
12. Hotlines - customized for large customers
13. Hot spares - customized for large customers, possibly consigned to them locally
14. Performance reporting - show uptime, scheduled maintenance, load factors, etc.
15. Usage and savings reporting - show cumulative efficiency and cost savings over time
16. Integration of information systems - now made much easier through internet collaboration tools
17. Dedicated account reps - inside and outside
18. Collaborative R&D - with customers and/or suppliers
19. Embedded support reps - based at large customer's location
20. Technology forecasts - tell them what's coming down the line, plan with them

21. Market research on customers' industries - tell them about developing trends, changing attitudes, new opportunities, etc.
22. Collaboration between executive management - council meetings, annual roundup events, conventions, user group meetings, symposiums, retreats, facility tours

If you look at these offerings from the standpoint of *you* as a customer, I know you'll agree that many would have value, and would lead you to select the supplier that offered them over one that did not (other things being the same). I have seen all of these offerings used with success. For example, in working collaboratively with a supplier on a new technology that we planned to use in a product, I wrote a technology forecast article that was picked up by a magazine, and eventually lead to a large sale to AT&T.

No business can survive a high customer churn rate. With trust, reliability, and appropriate sticky offerings, your ability to keep your customers happy and making referrals to others will go far to securing your future.

Differentiation Effectiveness Table

A useful way to look at your effective differentiation is to take your major niche markets and rank the purchase criteria that are most important to them. Start by ranking the top 4 criteria, and weight them in decreasing order from 10 to 7. You can expand the list if you like and change the weights, but the process is the same.

Next, rate your offering against your top competitor, using a 1 (lowest) to 10 (highest) scale, and multiply these figures by the appropriate weight of the purchase criteria. In the tables below are actual examples from a company that was struggling to grow. You can see it was lagging in differentiation in both Niche A and Niche B, and had let the competition out-maneuver them. It was particularly weak on price and variety.

*America has believed that in differentiation, not in uniformity, lies the path of progress.
It acted on this belief; it has advanced human happiness, and it has prospered.*

—Louis D. Brandeis

Niche A	Us	Competitor A
Importance Rank		
Variety (10x)	40	80
Price (9x)	45	63
Convenience (8x)	48	40
Quality (7x)	56	49
TOTAL SCORE	189	232

Niche B	Us	Competitor A
Importance Rank		
Quality (10x)	80	70
Convenience (9x)	54	45
Price (8x)	40	56
Variety (7x)	28	56
TOTAL SCORE	202	227

The next two tables show a "what if" change of strategy. By adding to variety and matching prices of Competitor A, differentiation would be back in our favor. Our advantages in convenience and quality would put us back on top.

Niche A	Us	Competitor A
Importance Rank		
Variety (10x)	**70**	80
Price (9x)	**63**	63
Convenience (8x)	48	40
Quality (7x)	56	49
TOTAL SCORE	237	232

Niche B	Us	Competitor A
Importance Rank		
Quality (10x)	80	70
Convenience (9x)	54	45
Price (8x)	**56**	56
Variety (7x)	**49**	56
TOTAL SCORE	239	227

📊 KEY TAKEAWAYS

- The keys to successful market entry are to:

  1. have a well identified customer who can be reached effectively
  2. specially target the top 20% of the customers in terms of buying power
  3. manage your cost of customer acquisition
  4. have an assortment of offers that will appeal to potential customers across the spectrum of awareness and interest levels in your solutions
  5. offer a deep assortment of customer stickiness services to keep your customers loyal and engaged to you
  6. strategically select your channel partners and foster a strong connection with them as an arm of your organization
  7. continually enhance the differentiation of your company from competitors in meaningful ways

- As you read these keys to success, you might be thinking, "Well, that's just common sense, right?" I can assure you that "common sense" is not common. Don't underestimate the power and value of these keys to success.

💡 TRY THIS

80/20 analysis of you market niches; customer stickiness list of offerings; market influencers chart; cost to acquire a customer; competitive differentiation table.

Summary

THIS IS A TIME WHEN IT HAS NEVER BEEN EASIER TO START A business. There is an increasing amount of support available through incubators, seed funds, and venture funds. It is also a time of threat from technological job displacement, global competition, terrorism, concerns of financial stability, etc.

You must stay on the offense though. The Foresight Method is a set of tools to keep you from wandering aimlessly, and help you answer the questions:

- How can the status quo be improved upon?
- What assumptions are no longer working?
- What new technological capabilities are likely to become available and how can they be useful?
- What newly emerging threats and risks do we need to be concerned about?
- What market trends do I expect to accelerate? What market trends are fading?
- In what ways are our customers changing?
- In what ways might we need to adapt our business platform and business model?
- In what ways can we make our products and services more novel, unique, and useful?
- What will be the greatest growth opportunities for the future?

In developing this method, my aim is to help you improve foresight about opportunities you can influence and participate in. You can start them at your current workplace, at a new workplace, or actively invest in them. The best way to start is to jump in to discovery. Start down the path, and soon ideas, contacts, inspiration, providence, and material assistance will come your way. Don't make a business decision right away. Most ideas are not viable as first stated, but you can improve them with feedback. Hopefully, you've learned

The secret of getting ahead is getting started.

—Mark Twain

here that the payback on reduction of uncertainty is very rewarding and well worth the effort.

Remember that foresight comes from being active in the flow of things; observing, discussing, researching, prototyping, hypothesizing, finding patterns, making notes, sketching ideas, experimenting, and testing. Don't work in a silo. Collaboration is critical. Foresight is intentional, it doesn't come from serendipity; it comes from a willful effort to engage with the world, especially your customers and target markets, in a methodical way.

It is crucial to sort dynamically, and to clarify major notions. In doing do you will expand the map of opportunities available to you. This is the crux of the method. You must insist on high quality concepts to rate and rank for further pursuit. Incremental improvement is not the goal. Use the rating and ranking tool to focus on your 40+ rated concepts. These have great potential returns.

Use the simple statistical tools to improve your decision making. If you don't have the insights to fill in the blanks yet, that tells you something valuable, right? It means you are in a state of uncertainty, and you never want to proceed in those circumstances.

You don't need a final finished product to test in the market. In fact, it is better to wait until you get feedback before locking in design constraints, because you might need to make a radical change that would become expensive and cause major delays. With software and apps, you can test with wire frames, products can be shown with animated CAD and 3D prints. You can simulate performance with bits and pieces cobbled together from existing products.

Armed with a well-stated premise, you can solicit useful feedback that greatly improves your likelihood of success. Be realistic about your market projections, have your facts in line, and be cognizant of possible overconfidence in your probability assessments. Perhaps the biggest "wrench" to get thrown into your plans will come from unforeseen competition. If you have success, your offering will be noticed by competitors quickly. Unless it is relatively difficult to copy, you can expect pressure from them, so best to be prepared and start working on version 2 sooner than later. Ideally, you will secure patent or copyright protection as soon as possible.

If starting a new venture of your own is not to your liking, the tools here are useful for you to bring foresight to your current place of work. Or perhaps you will identify a potential employer in a new area you have explored. Certainly, the insights you have gained and the opportunities you have identified will make you more valuable to employers. Also, it could help you to make better investment choices. Whatever your path, make it upward.

NOTES

1   Alfred North Whitehead, mathematician and philosopher, is the defining figure of process philosophy. This book has adapted a number of his concepts such as: foresight; flow; emergence; speculation; novelty; effective contrast; fatigue; and method. See Whitehead's books, *The Concept of Nature* (1920), *Process and Reality* (1929), and, *Adventures of Ideas* (1933). Also see *Process-Relational Philosophy* (2008) by C. Robert Mesle.

2   See https://www.accenture.com/lv-en/_acnmedia/PDF-33/Accenture-Why-AI-is-the-Future-of-Growth.pdf.

3   *Dr. Spencer Johnson wrote *Who Moved My Cheese* (1998).

4   These primary strategic options are identified by Bain consultants James Allen and Chris Zook in an article *Growth Outside the Core*, Harvard Business Review, December 2003.

5   "Corporate Longevity: Turbulence Ahead for Large Organizations" (see https://www.innosight.com/insight/corporate-longevity-turbulence-ahead-for-large-organizations/).

6   This formula is from Kazuo Inamori, Japanese business executive and entrepreneur.

7   Darwin, C. R. Notebook B: [Transmutation of species (1837-1838)]. CUL-DAR121.-Transcribed by Kees Rookmaaker. (*Darwin Online*, http://darwin-online.org.uk/).

8   Christian Gottfried Ehrenberg. *Die fossilen Infusorien und die lebendige Dammerde*, Berlin 1837.

9   Richard Owen. Probably personal communication.

10   Source: Darwin letter to J.S. Henslow, his mentor, written during his discovery voyage on the Beagle.

11   *The Da Vinci Notebooks at sacred-texts.com.*

12   This formula is from venture capital firm Kleiner Perkins.

13   *See www.howtomeasureanything.com.*

About the Author

SCOTT BARNETT CREATES TOOLS AND METHODS to support executives in adapting their businesses to changing customer demands and competitive threats. His insights from 30 years of marketing research, product management, marketing and sales management, consulting, and entrepreneurship are embedded in the 7-step *Profiting from Foresight* method that increases: focus on productive activities, innovative impact on customers, accountability, and profits.

Customers are switching loyalty to businesses that empower them to take control of costs, variety, delivery, speed, customization, payment, mobility, etc. Scott has found it crucial for businesses to anticipate technological progress, and to foresee how to enhance their capabilities to profitably empower increasingly demanding customers. His long-term record of successful ventures and launches proves the method's power to help a team expand its vision of what is possible, and develop purposeful plans of action to meet new demands.

Scott has worked for, and advised, businesses ranging in size from Fortune 500 companies to new startups. One of his notable achievements was turning around a technology company that was near bankruptcy to become the most profitable in its sector. The strategies that saved this company were unconventional, but successful, due to foresight about attractive growth paths that were emerging. Scott's foresight method identifies missing pieces of the puzzle to add new capability, bridge into new markets, and reduce the risk of innovation.

Scott graduated from the business program at Miami University, Oxford, OH, and has an MBA from Case Western Reserve University in Cleveland, OH. He and his family reside in the Chicago metro area.

To contact Scott, please email to: sbarnett@better-faster.com

 If you enjoyed this book, we would appreciate it if you would post a review of it on Amazon to let others know of its value to you.

Made in United States
North Haven, CT
04 December 2021